HOME DESIGN WORKBOOKS
BATHROOM

HOME DESIGN WORKBOOKS
BATHROOM

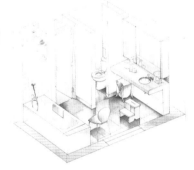

S U Z A N N E   A R D L E Y

DK PUBLISHING, INC.

A DK PUBLISHING BOOK

Project Editor BELLA PRINGLE
Project Art Editor SHARON MOORE
US Editor RAY ROGERS
DTP Designer MARK BRACEY
Photography JAKE FITZJONES
Stylist FIONA CRAIG-MCFEELY
Production Controller ALISON JONES
Series Editor CHARLOTTE DAVIES
Series Art Editor CLIVE HAYBALL

First American Edition, 1998
4 6 8 10 9 7 5
Published in the United States by DK Publishing, Inc.
95 Madison Avenue, New York, New York 10016
www.dk.com
Copyright © 1998 Dorling Kindersley Limited, London
Text copyright © 1998 Suzanne Ardley

Library of Congress Cataloging-in-Publication Data
    Ardley, Suzanne.
    Bathroom / Suzanne Ardley. -- Ist American ed.
    p.   cm. -- (Home design workbooks)
    Includes index.
    ISBN 0–7894–3526–8
    1. Bathroom. 2. Interior decoration. I. Title.
    II. Series: DK home design workbooks.
NK2117.B33Y37 1998
747.7'8--dc21

Text film output in Great Britain by R & B Creative Services Ltd
Reproduced in Singapore by Pica
Printed and bound in China by L.Rex Printing Co., Ltd.

INTRODUCTION • 6

BATHROOM ELEMENTS • 20

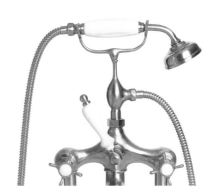

CONTENTS

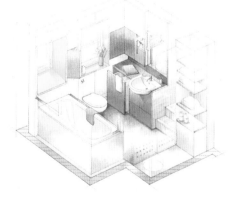

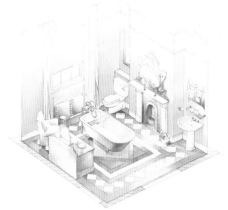

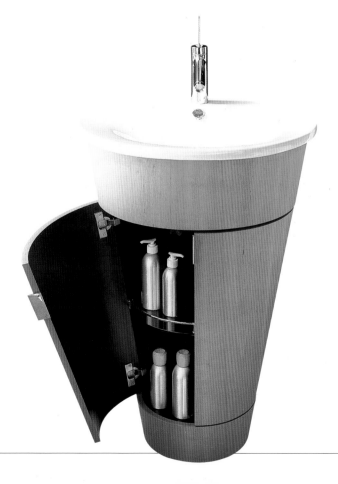

INTRODUCTION

△ **PRIMITIVE SHOWER**
Taking a shower rather
than a bath was considered
eccentric when this portable
shower was made in the
1800s. The innovative
design has a tank supported
by mock bamboo poles and,
on pulling the lever, water
is released through the fixed
shower head and collects
in the foot bowl.

THE BATHROOM is probably the most
personal and private room in the house
and one that is in frequent use. The
success of a bathroom design relies on taking
into account the demands that will be made on
the room. Will it be a functional bathroom for a
busy family, or a luxurious room, purely for one's
own use, in which to relax? Bathrooms are no
longer regarded simply as utilitarian washrooms
where cleansing rituals are performed out of
sight behind closed doors. They are congenial
spaces where you can surround yourself with
well-designed, practical, and aesthetic objects
that reflect both your lifestyle and taste.

More than ever, people expect bathrooms
to fulfill a range of functions and are happy to
remodel the existing bathroom, convert a spare
room into a bathroom, or add a bathroom so
that they can indulge in everything from a
bracing wake-up shower or soothing hot spa
to the exclusivity of a bathroom-cum-dressing
room. Even where space is tight, clever planning
and positioning of fixtures can ensure time spent
in the bathroom is truly pleasurable.

BATHROOM INFLUENCES

My initial interest in bathroom design was
awakened by a visit to Fiji some years ago when
visiting old family friends in the Nausoris. Their
remote Colonial-style house had a wonderfully
simple but effective shower system. Fed by a
rainwater tank hidden in the treetops, ice-cold
water coursed through a hose to a colossal
shower head towering above the stall. No half-
way measures here: plunging into the deluge,

▽ **BATHING IN GRANDEUR**
Kingston Lacy was one of the first stately homes in England to install a bathroom on a grand scale. Before plumbing was installed in the 1920s, servants filled the bathtub and washstand with hot water.

◁ **BOLD AND SIMPLE**
Simple lines and uncluttered surfaces are the mainstay of modern bathroom design. Durable, low-maintenance materials are perfect for busy people with limited time for keeping the bathroom spotlessly clean.

you were left gasping and drenched in cold water from head to toe. Having experienced my first invigorating "power shower," I was convinced that showers were as therapeutic as they were cleansing and, on my return to England, tried to recreate the same showering experience.

EARLY WASHING FACILITIES

In stark contrast to the old saying "cleanliness is next to Godliness," early domestic washing facilities were as basic, but less effective, than my shower in Fiji and consisted of a bowl and a pitcher of water placed in a corner of the bedroom. There were no bathrooms, but, on occasion, a portable bathtub was brought into the room and filled by hand with water heated on the fire. Family members would take turns bathing in the same water. It was impractical to take a bath on a daily basis, so odors were masked with scents such as lavender, bergamot, and rosemary.

1930s BATHROOM ▷
Demand for bathroom facilities grew in the 1930s, which led to a wider choice of fixtures, including this type of simple pedestal sink; colored rather than white fixtures were considered to be luxury items.

△ **RETRO LOOK**
Modern technology joins forces here with classic 1930s style to give a heated towel rack that looks good and works efficiently.

By the mid-1800s, specifically built bathrooms began to be installed, but only in grander houses. These bathrooms were furnished comfortably like other rooms in the house, but instead of displaying elegant bureaus and dining tables, they had ornate washstands, dressing tables, and bathtubs. These early bathrooms helped the rich distinguish themselves from the "great unwashed," at a time when people began to understand that dirt carried germs and potentially fatal diseases.

FORM AND STYLE

In time, soft furnishings and ornate details were considered inappropriate for bathrooms since they gather dust, and so the room evolved a colder, more clinical appearance. Plain white tubs and metal hardware became the norm.

By the 1940s, pressed-steel tubs with hand-held showers were being mass produced, enabling more homes to own a bathtub, but, aside from some patterned porcelain and plain-colored fixtures, bathrooms remained functional.

BATHROOM COLORS

The 1970s and 1980s saw a dazzling array of colored fixtures and unusual tub shapes fueled by a desire for exclusivity, while near the turn of this century, the minimalist metal, glass, and mosaic designs reign supreme. Despite the hi-tech movement, traditional fixtures and hardware have undergone a revival with roll-top tubs, classic brass shower heads, dark mahogany paneling, and ornate furnishings becoming increasingly popular. Modern reproductions abound, but, for lovers of authenticity, original fixtures are available, restored to their former glory by specialist retailers. Faucets and handles, ball-jointed radiators, and wrought-iron clothes horses complete this nostalgic dip into the past, re-creating its own distinct and decadent style.

ADDITIONAL FACILITIES

Today, a comfortable bathroom is taken for granted, and now in family homes we have come to expect a second bathroom or a separate shower room to prevent a bottleneck of users at peak times. House builders appreciate this trend, and second bathrooms, particularly an incorporated bathroom or shower room leading off the master bedroom, are fast becoming a standard specification for new homes. Property developers and real-estate agents agree that an extra bathroom increases both the desirability and value of your home.

The popularity of the second bathroom has also been fueled by the development of space-saving fixture designs and ventilation systems. It is now possible to fit most facilities into the smallest of spaces – a feat that would have been impossible in the past.

INNOVATIVE DESIGN

Bathroom design has now become a state-of-the-art industry, combining form and function with the latest technology. In addition to a huge choice of bathtubs and showers, and bath/shower modules, a spectacular range of fixtures offers

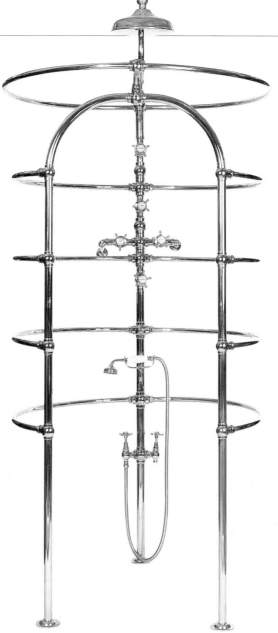

◁ **NEEDLE SHOWER 1910**
Early enthusiasts of showers would have been impressed by this striking design with its overhead shower head and a series of body sprays from the circular tubes that created the first all-around shower.

▽ **JACUZZI SHOWER**
Showers over bathtubs are not new, but Jacuzzi's all-in-one system is designed to fit into the space of a standard bathtub. The power shower capsule and sleek shape make bathing highly enjoyable.

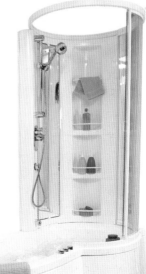

hydrotherapy, steam cleansing, lymph stimulation, and body-toning systems. The introduction to the industry of ceramic disk technology enables a single-lever mixer, with just one handle and spout, to deliver an even temperature and flow of water. The ceramic disk creates an ultra-smooth action as you turn the faucet on and off, the mixer does not drip, and it resists scale buildup in hard-water areas. Booster pumps have also had their part to play by improving water pressure and overall shower performance. Water temperatures can now be preset for adults and children, while, as an additional safety measure, unbearably hot water from the shower head will cut out instantly to prevent scalding. These small but highly significant developments in bathroom technology have transformed the face of the ordinary bathroom, making it more efficient, safe, and fun to use.

ENVIRONMENTAL CONCERNS

In response to the arrival of new bathroom materials, finishes, and hardware, manufacturers have developed a host of cleaning chemicals to keep your bathroom in pristine condition. There are products that prevent and remove scale deposits, chemicals that dissolve residue left by soaps and oils, and substances to eradicate stubborn mildew. But the use of these harsh chemicals, combined with the dramatic increase in the amount of water required by each household to sustain more than one bathroom, is creating serious environmental problems. Responsible manufacturers are addressing these issues by developing products, especially toilet tanks, that use less water to flush than models currently in production. At present, 1.6 gallons (7.5 liters) of water are needed to flush the toilet; with improvements in design, this is likely to be reduced in the near future.

Much can be done by individuals to save water when using the bathroom on a daily basis. Remember, a shower uses up much less water than running a full tub so, if possible, try to take more showers. Another small but important step is to remember to turn off the faucet rather than

△ CONTEMPORARY FAUCET
Ceramic disk technology has led to single-lever faucets that control both the flow rate and temperature mix of the water smoothly and effortlessly.

leaving it running while brushing your teeth. Also ensure that faucets do not drip: a huge amount of water can be wasted this way.

PLANNING YOUR BATHROOM

Many bathrooms are as intensively planned and as expensive to install as kitchens; the plumbing and drainage pipes, wiring, sockets, and heating and ventilation systems all need to be accurately placed within the room and must comply with health and safety regulations.

When designing the space, aim to arrive at a solution that suits your lifestyle. Consider what demands will be made on the bathroom, how much time will be spent in it, and who will use it. The time you devote to this, and assessing the advantages and disadvantages of bathroom hardware, will be rewarded when you emerge from a room that leaves you feeling a hundred times better than when you went in.

△ MODERN MATERIALS
The combination of durable stainless steel, a clear acrylic toilet seat that is warm to the touch, and a hidden water tank produces a well-considered toilet design.

WHAT DO YOU WANT FROM YOUR BATHROOM?

Before purchasing a group of expensive fixtures and hardware, analyze your lifestyle and bathing habits and decide which family members are going to use the new bathroom. To help you arrive at a solution, compare the benefits of the bathroom facilities below.

❶ A space that can be shared with others.

❷ A bathroom equipped with child-safety features.

❸ A room that doubles up as a dressing room.

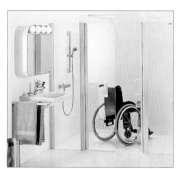

❹ Facilities that less-abled people can easily use.

❺ A comfortably furnished bathroom in which to relax.

❻ A fitted bathroom where everything can be put away.

❼ A bathroom that makes the best use of a small area.

❽ A shower room rather than a bathroom.

❾ Maximum comfort from existing facilities.

HOW CAN THIS SPACE WORK FOR YOU?

Whatever the shape or size of your bathroom, you will want to get the most from the products you choose. Decide how suitable the room is for the items you wish to include and what alterations, if any, will be required.
☐ Is your present bathroom big enough for you and your family's needs, or would converting a spare bedroom into a large bathroom be a better planning solution?
☐ Would choosing compact fixture designs enable you to squeeze a shower, bathtub, and other items into a limited space, or would a separate shower room someplace else in your home be a more satisfactory solution?
☐ Is the bathroom lighting good enough to see by when shaving or applying cosmetics, or could it be improved by a second window or specialized lighting around the mirror or sink area?

CHOOSING A STYLE ▷
This fresh white bathroom combines a range of simple style details that are subtly coordinated. Little touches, such as family photos, fresh flowers, and a terracotta pot holding toilet paper, present an elegant but well-furnished look.

△ FORM AND FUNCTION
High-quality hardware will enhance the performance and the look of ordinary items of sanitaryware. Choose an eye-catching design combined with a simple, smooth operation.

The style choices you make for your bathroom are personal and need to be carefully thought through. Your selection of products is crucial. Fixtures and hardware must last well and still look good after several years' wear and tear. To help you decide which elements you wish to include in your brand-new or remodeled bathroom, establish what you like and dislike about the existing room. Ask yourself questions such as: How easy is it to step in and out of the tub? How warm is the bathroom on cold winter mornings? Are the fixtures easy to clean? Is the shower powerful enough? Also, consider the architectural features in the room itself, such as decorative plasterwork and the windows, and how they will affect the finished look. Before pulling everything out and starting from scratch, stop to ask whether some of the existing elements might fit equally well with the style of your new bathroom plan.

STYLE PREFERENCES

Regarding my own personal style, as much as I love the simplicity of contemporary bathroom design and innovative new materials, I feel most comfortable in rooms that have an informal,

◁ CHOOSING THE ELEMENTS
Look for attractive designs that also help with
your storage. This modern pedestal sink has a
compartment for storing towels and a ledge on
which to rest soaps when washing your hands.

out of reach of young children and, if you
choose a back-to-wall toilet, the tank will be
boxed in behind a half-height false wall or
tongue-and-groove paneling creating a display
shelf on top for attractive bottles and jars.

CHARACTER AND FUNCTION

Once you have decided which style you favor,
look for fixtures, materials, and hardware that
will add the desired character but are, above all,
functional. Collect manufacturers' brochures
outlining the specification of each product
to help you make informed decisions. In the
chapter featuring *Bathroom Elements*, both the
advantages and disadvantages of the major
bathroom products are outlined. For example,
if you have young children, you will be able to
judge whether ceramic tiles or rubber flooring is
best. Whatever element you are considering, take

ived-in atmosphere. Objects that are displayed
because you like them, or simply because they
have been handed down to you, achieve a warm
personal look that others, selected merely to
present an image, often lack. In the same way,
a clever blend of contemporary and traditional
pieces can produce spectacular results, so even
if your bathroom is in an old house, do not feel
limited to furnishing it with period pieces.

Whatever your style preferences, try to plan
as much storage space as possible in your new
bathroom so that items do not clutter up
countertops and other activity areas. Place only
attractive objects on display, and keep utilitarian
items hidden behind closed doors. Toiletries,
toilet paper, cleaning materials, medicines, and
first-aid boxes take up considerable space.
Installing a semicountertop sink, with storage
units beneath, is one solution. Shelves around
the walls at shoulder height can be used to
display decorative accessories while keeping them

WHAT COULD YOU CHANGE?

Use the following
checklist to help you
pinpoint what it is
about your bathroom
that you would like
to improve or replace.
☐ Change shape of
existing room.
☐ Alter architectural
features.
☐ Improve access to
natural light.
☐ Upgrade fixtures and
hardware.
☐ Renew tiling and
waterproof seals.
☐ Replace flooring.
☐ Redesign lighting.
☐ Add shaving sockets.
☐ Improve ventilation
and heating.
☐ Reorganize plumbing.
☐ Reduce noise levels.
☐ Increase privacy.
☐ Reorganize available
storage space.
☐ Rethink the size,
height, and position
of bathroom fixtures.
☐ Change furniture.
☐ Update all curtains,
blinds, and other soft
furnishings.

◁ CHOOSING DETAILS
Most bathroom bottles,
pots, containers, and tubes
are small. Plan separate shelf
compartments so items can
be stored and found easily.
Mirror-fronted cabinets
also reflect light. Choose a
lockable design to protect
children from danger.

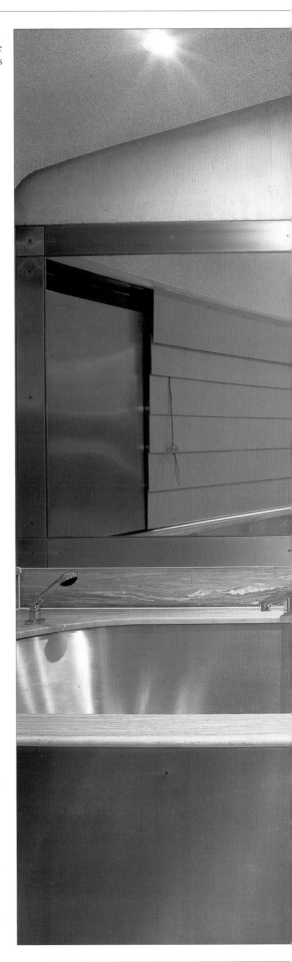

PLAN OF ACTION

Having decided on the
style and elements you
wish to include, use this
checklist before starting
alterations to ensure
that nothing has
been overlooked.

☐ Have you received
permission from the
relevant authorities for
additional plumbing
fixtures or received
consent for structural
alterations?

☐ Will you need the
help of professionals,
or will you be able to
do most of the work
yourself?

☐ Are you planning to
renovate or re-enamel
fixtures, for example, a
cast-iron bathtub? Do
you need help having
it taken out?

☐ Have you costed the
total job and received
quotes for the work you
cannot do yourself?

☐ Have you allowed a
little extra money in the
budget for finishing
decoration and soft
furnishings?

into account its practicality in a bathroom
environment because daily contact with heat,
steam, and splashes of water soon cause inferior
materials to deteriorate.

It is not just the fixtures that need to be
attractive and functional in bathrooms but also
the lighting, wallcoverings, window treatments,
furniture, and cabinet surfaces. Good lighting
makes a bathroom safer to use; well-chosen
flooring will be both durable and comfortable
underfoot; and the right cabinet finish can
transform the look of the bathroom and offer
a water-resistant surface. These considerations
present an opportunity to influence the look
of the room while achieving a comfortable
bathroom that is simple to maintain.

IDEAS INTO REALITY

This book is intended to help you to arrive at
an ergonomic design with items arranged for
ease of use and visual pleasure.

If your bathroom plans are ambitious – for
example, if the room needs to be extended to
accommodate the fixtures or you are adding a
second bathroom in the attic – you should also
consult a qualified architect. An architect will
want to look at your proposed bathroom before
start of work so that he or she can advise you
on building regulations, and he will also be able
to recommend plumbers, fitters, and electricians
and will organize every detail of the job from
beginning to end. Architects will be able to
inspect ongoing work to ensure it is of a
satisfactory standard and on schedule. If you
want to create a bathroom that satisfies all your
needs, however, your input is vital, so use the
following pages to help you formulate your
design ideas before putting them into practice.

HOW THIS BOOK WORKS

THIS BOOK gives you the practical know-how you need to design a bathroom that matches your lifestyle and to create an efficient and comfortable space. It will help you plan a new bathroom or adapt an existing one. A series of questions helps you assess what you need from your bathroom, then a survey of fixtures and hardware helps you choose the right elements for your room. Next, three-dimensional plans of seven bathrooms explain how to engineer successful designs. Finally, there are instructions on drawing up a bathroom plan.

2. SELECT COMPONENTS ▽

To help you compile a list of the features that will best suit your requirements, a range of fixtures, hardware, and furniture are surveyed (*pp. 20–45*). A "remember" box draws your attention to important design points, and the advantages and disadvantages of each element are discussed. Simple diagrams demonstrate how to use and where to position your fixtures and furniture for maximum safety, comfort, and efficiency.

1. IDENTIFY YOUR NEEDS ▽

A number of preliminary questions (*pp. 18–19*) are asked to encourage you to think about your bathroom needs and the suitability and potential of your type of bathroom. By examining aspects of your personal and family life, such as how often you bathe or shower, you will find it easier to identify the most suitable fixtures and most appropriate design solutions.

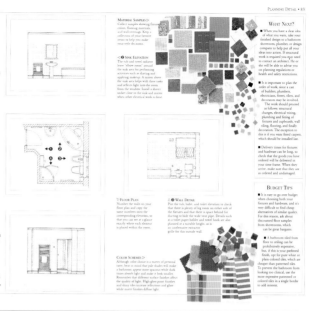

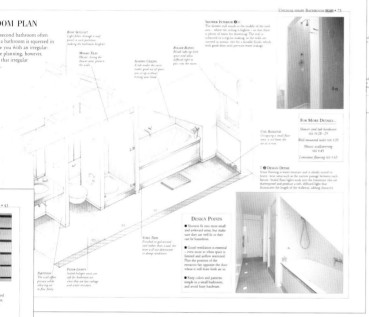

4. DESIGN YOUR BATHROOM △

When you feel satisfied with your own bathroom ideas, turn to *Plan Your Design* (*pp.76–83*) and put your design thoughts into practice. This section provides step-by-step instructions for measuring the room intended for your bathroom, plus details on how to draw the floor plan and different elevations to scale. Common design mistakes are pinpointed, and successful solutions are shown and explained.

3. LEARN HOW TO PLAN △

A chapter on *Room Plans* (*pp.46–75*) looks in detail at seven existing bathroom designs and offers advice and inspiration on how to bring together all the elements in your own plan, whether you are designing a brand-new bathroom or remodeling an existing one. A three-dimensional drawing, a bird's-eye-view plan, photographs, and a list of design points explain the thinking behind each of the seven design solutions.

HOW TO USE THE GRAPH PAPER

■ Draw up your room to scale (*pp.78–79*) using the graph paper provided (*pp.89–96*). You may photocopy it if you need more.

■ For a bathroom with small dimensions, use the graph paper with an imperial scale of 1:24, where one large square represents 1ft and one small square represents 3in. Or, use the metric scale of 1:20, where one large square represents 1m and a small square 10cm. For example, an area 10ft long is drawn across ten large squares.

■ For a larger bathroom, use the imperial graph paper with the smaller scale of 1:48. The large square represents 4ft and the small squares 6in. Or, use the metric graph paper with the scale 1:50, where a large square equals 1m and a small square just 10cm.

■ Having plotted your room, try various designs on a tracing paper overlay.

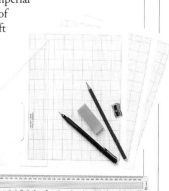

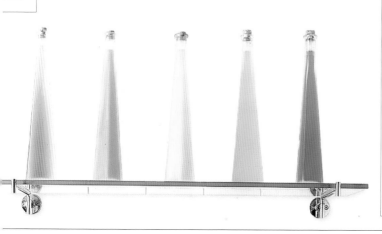

ASSESS YOUR NEEDS

THE FOLLOWING questions will help you focus on your specific bathroom needs and think about ways to approach bathroom planning so that, as you work through the book, you will be able to compile a list of the bathroom elements and designs that best suit you and your lifestyle.

TUBS AND HARDWARE

Consider the amount of time you like to spend in the bathtub and whether you prefer a quick dip, a long soak, or a tub that doubles up as a shower. Think about the needs of other members of the family and whether you would like a tub that is large enough to share. These decisions will help you decide on the size and type of bathtub you need, plus the best hardware and a suitable location within the room.

■ BATHTUBS
☐ Would fitting a corner, tapered, or compact bathtub free up much-needed space along one wall for an extra fixture, such as a toilet or bidet?
☐ Do you like to spend time lying back and relaxing in the tub? If so, have you considered designs that will cradle your head, neck, and back in comfort?
☐ If you do a strenuous job that leaves you with aching muscles, would a whirlpool or spa system be a good idea?
☐ Do you enjoy taking a long time in the tub? If so, would you like to be sure that your chosen bathtub material retains the heat well? Or would a heated bathtub panel be useful?
☐ Would you like the bathtub to double up as shower? Does the base of the bath have an nonslip surface for safety?
☐ Is easy maintenance important to you? Remember, baths in dark colors lose their looks quickly in hard-water areas since scale deposits mark the surface.
☐ Do you like to share a bathtub with someone else? If so, will any structural alterations be necessary to strengthen the bathroom floor?
☐ Do you have young children or less-able family members who would find climbing into a bathtub difficult? Would they benefit from safety grab bars?

■ BATHTUB HARDWARE
☐ Are your children likely to pull out the tub stopper? Would attached hardware be more practical than a plug and chain?
☐ When different members of the family take turns using the bathtub as a shower, would a bathtub/shower mixer with a temperature guard be a wise choice to avoid possible scalding from hot water?
☐ Do you wish to be able to wash your hair while in the bathtub? If so, have you chosen a bath/shower mixer that will suit the rim of your chosen bath?
☐ Do you have young or elderly family members who find it difficult to operate faucet handles? Have you considered lever handles, which are easier to use?

SHOWERS

An effective shower needs to be carefully planned to work with your existing plumbing system. Consider how many times a day you want to shower and whether you would like to have different showering options, such as a massage setting. Think about the people who will use the shower and whether you need safety features for the young or elderly. Also, consider whether it is easier to house the shower in a separate room.

☐ Do you want the convenience of instant hot water for showers at any time of the day or night, or do your showering times correspond with the availability of hot water from the hot water tank?
☐ Do you prefer a powerful shower? If so, is it possible to install a shower pump to improve the shower's performance?
☐ If there is sufficient space, would a large double shower, enabling you to bend and stretch without touching the sides when washing, appeal to you?
☐ Would a shower that can double up as a relaxing steam room suit your lifestyle?
☐ If you opt for a shower with body jets, can the position of the jets be altered to suit all the family members who use it?
☐ Are there less-able members of the family who will find stepping in and out of the shower difficult? Would they view a built-in shower seat as a practical addition?
☐ Have you dismissed installing a shower stall because space in the bathroom is restricted? Did you know that shower stalls can be installed with a choice of inward and sliding doors that use space only within the shower stall to open?
☐ Would you prefer an invigorating shower with needle jets of water, a relaxing shower with massage and pulse options, or one that offers a choice of functions to suit all members of the family?

☐ Do you like to be drenched from head to toe in water, or would an adjustable shower head that can be raised or lowered to target different parts of your body without getting your hair wet each time be more useful?
☐ Do you like to keep soap and shampoo within the shower enclosure? Would a shower stall with a space designed to hold these items be useful?

SINKS AND HARDWARE

Make your choice of sink and hardware simple by considering the people who will be using the sink on a daily basis. Decide whether more than one person will want to have access to a sink at the same time. Will you be carrying out other activities, such as shaving and hair-washing? This will influence the height of the sink and position of the hardware.

☐ Will two people want to wash in the bathroom at the same time? Have you the space to fit twin sinks with enough elbow room for two people?
☐ Do you require space under the sink to store items? Would a wall-mounted sink help free up this floor area?
☐ Are you taller or smaller than average? Would it be more comfortable to fit a wall-mounted sink at a height that suits you? If so, have you checked that the wall sink you have chosen can be fitted with a cover to hide the pipework or recess the supply pipes in the wall?
☐ Do you have young children who tend to overfill the sink or splash water onto the floor? Would a sink with inward sloping edges be a good idea to prevent spillage onto the floor?
☐ Do you want to wash your hair in the sink? If so, can the faucet be turned to the side so that your head can fit quite comfortably in the sink?

TOILETS AND BIDETS

Think carefully about who will use the toilet and bidet, how often, and for how long. The most important factors are comfort and cleanliness. Other points worth considering when selecting a toilet are how easy is it to operate the flush mechanism, how much water the toilet needs to flush, and whether you want a close-coupled, low-level, or high tank.

☐ Does the toilet seat rest against the tank or wall when open to prevent it from falling shut at any moment?
☐ Will both young and older members of the household be able to sit down and stand up from the toilet with ease?
☐ Would you prefer to mount the toilet bowl on the wall so that the seat can be higher or lower than average?
☐ Are the toilet bowl, seat hinges, water inlet, and rim easy to clean?
☐ Do you want to conserve water? Is there a choice of different flushing modes with the tank, for example a half-press for a short flush or a full press for a long flush of water?
☐ If you want an old-fashioned, high-level tank, does the bathroom have tall walls to enable the tank to sit high above the toilet so that the force of water is strong enough to flush the toilet?

STORAGE

Make a mental list of the type of items you would like to keep in the bathroom. If it is a family bathroom, take account of products that will need to be stored out of reach of children. The type and amount of storage space you need to design into your bathroom will be determined by the number of products you and your family use and who requires access to these products.

☐ Do you have enough cupboard space to house your beauty and cleaning products?
☐ Could the storage of everyday items be better planned so that less-used items do not obstruct access to those you use regularly?
☐ Do you want storage cupboards that are easy to maintain in a bathroom setting? If so, have you checked that the cabinet finishes are steamproof and the hinges rustproof?
☐ Do you want a bathroom cabinet that can be locked so that medicines and cleaning chemicals can be kept away from children?
☐ Do you need a container for storing children's bathtub toys?

BATHROOM ELEMENTS

BATHTUB SHAPES

MAKING SURE THAT A BATHTUB is a pleasure to use is as important as how it looks. Before coming to a decision, ask permission to climb in and out of the tubs you like on your showroom visits; although you may feel ridiculous, it is the only way to check that you can use the tub easily. Once in a bathtub, see that it suits your body shape by stretching out your legs and reaching for the handles. Check that accessories, such as grab bars, are well placed.

POPULAR SHAPES

The rectangular tub is still the most popular shape, partly because it fits neatly into a bathroom corner and also because of its practical lines, which enable the occupant to stretch out and lie down. From this basic shape, a range of modern space-saving designs have evolved, such as the tapered bathtub. For a traditional style, the vintage bathtub (*below*) or double-ended bathtub (*below right*) are comfortable and good-looking designs.

△ **STANDARD BATHTUB**
The addition of a nonslip step, grab bar, and shelf unit to a standard rectangular bathtub is worth considering for a family bathroom.

▽ **VINTAGE BATHTUB**
Position freestanding bathtubs so that there is plenty of space around them to show off their contours and to enable you to step in and out of the bathtub from either side.

BATHTUB RACK
Essential for holding washing items where wall-mounted dishes are impractical.

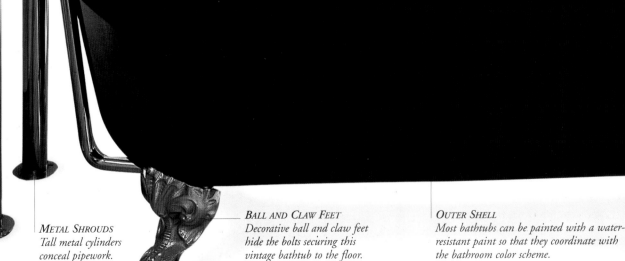

METAL SHROUDS
Tall metal cylinders conceal pipework.

BALL AND CLAW FEET
Decorative ball and claw feet hide the bolts securing this vintage bathtub to the floor.

OUTER SHELL
Most bathtubs can be painted with a water-resistant paint so that they coordinate with the bathroom color scheme.

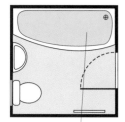

A tapered end creates space for other elements.

◁ TAPERED BATHTUB

A clever and practical solution to cramped bathroom conditions is to install a tapered tub, which gives more space where it is needed – at the end where you stand up and shower. Meanwhile, the narrow end allows space beside it for a full-size sink with elbow room; the sink can be used in comfort without hitting the tub edge.

*INNER SURFACE
Enameled surfaces are durable but colder to touch than acrylic.*

ELBOW ROOM

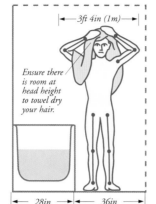

←— 3ft 4in (1m) —→

Ensure there is room at head height to towel dry your hair.

←28in→ ←36in→

Plan a floor area at least 36in (90cm) wide alongside the tub so that you can towel dry both the upper and lower half of your body in comfort.

REMEMBER

■ Access to all bathroom plumbing is essential. Ensure that paneled bath surrounds on rectangular bathtubs can be opened quickly in an emergency by fitting either magnetic catches or hinges.

■ Abrasive cleaning liquids and chemicals can damage acrylic and enameled bathtub surfaces and shorten their life. Use only products recommended by the bathtub manufacturer.

■ To make the bathtub safe for young and old people, install grab bars and nonslip mats.

△ DOUBLE-ENDED BATHTUB

Comfortable ends and centered plumbing are essential if the tub is for more than one. The tub should be deep enough to prevent displaced water from overflowing.

ALTERNATIVE SHAPES

Manufacturers also produce tubs in rounded shapes. A circular or corner bathtub may be more in keeping with your bathing needs, especially if you enjoy sharing a bath with your partner or tend to bathe several children at once. It may fit more successfully into your room plan than a rectangular bathtub.

△ ▷ FULL CIRCLE

Most round tubs have a greater water capacity than standard shapes, so they take longer to fill up and are less economical. They are usually manufactured from acrylic or fiberglass, which makes them light, and a shelf-seat is molded into the design for comfort and ease of use.

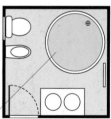

A round tub leaves space for other essential items.

◁ △ CORNER BATHTUB

A tub tucked into a corner occupies a similar floor area to a standard tub but fills the space differently, which can be an advantage when planning a bathroom layout; a corner tub is shorter than a standard one, so an extra item can be placed next to it along one wall.

This design leaves space for a radiator to warm towels.

SPECIALIZED BATHTUBS

FOR THOSE WHO PERCEIVE bathing as a special time to indulge in the therapeutic effects of water, there is a whole host of sophisticated systems that can both stimulate and relax you. Alternatively, you may prefer to plunge into a gleaming copper tub or submerge yourself in a deep pool of water.

TONING AND RELAXING

The therapeutic properties of whirlpools and similar bathtubs are undeniable. They offer a perfect way to unwind at the end of the day. A stream of water mixed with air is pumped out of jets to massage the neck, back, thighs, and feet, encouraging good circulation.

WHIRLPOOL AND SHOWER UNIT ▷
Combining a whirlpool with an invigorating shower in one compact unit makes good use of limited space. It also eliminates the need for extra plumbing that two self-contained systems require. The circular end provides room to shower in comfort, with shelves for shampoo and soaps.

WATER THERAPY
The speed of the jets can be altered for a relaxing or invigorating body massage.

◁ WHIRLPOOL
To ensure the muscles really benefit and relax, the water in the whirlpool should be deep enough to lightly support the weight of the body. The water should be warm, not uncomfortably hot, to encourage a total sense of well-being.

TEMPERATURE CONTROL
A thermostat keeps the heat constant.

MULTISPRAY HEAD
Delivers a soothing puls of water or energizing j

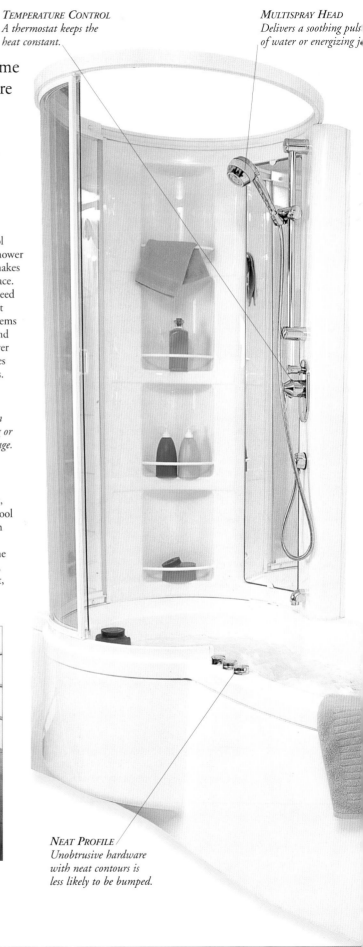

NEAT PROFILE
Unobtrusive hardware with neat contours is less likely to be bumped.

△ **HYDROTHERAPY**
A sculptured headrest and sloping back gently support the body, aiding the jets of aerated water to massage directly along the length of the spine. A touch-control pad within arm's reach can alter the waterflow and also the temperature to maintain comfort levels throughout the treatment.

SIT BATHTUBS

Sit tubs take up less floor space than standard bathtubs but keep you in an upright bathing position. Although this sounds awkward, it can be very soothing; these bathtubs are often so deep that you can submerge yourself up to your neck in water. Taller than standard tubs, they can be difficult to fit into small spaces.

TELEPHONE HANDSET
Traditional hardware, mounted on the tub rim, adds character.

◁ **HIP BATHTUBS**
Designed to be used for a quick wash rather than a long soak, a hip bathtub uses a small amount of space and water.

STEP DETAIL
Natural wood steps help you climb over the steep side.

SMALL PROPORTIONS
A neat shape that is suited to bathrooms where the tub has only occasional use.

DEEP TUB ▷
Two people can sit comfortably on the recessed seat in this deep tub. Finished in natural wood, the resin construction is both strong and lightweight, and the hardware is neat and unobtrusive.

REMEMBER

■ The weight of a large, full tub can be enormous. Check that the floor is strong enough to support the tub when filled with water and occupants.

■ The use of bath oils or foam is not advised in spa baths since they clog up the small aeration holes and produce a mass of bubbles. Have the jets checked and serviced regularly.

■ Wood and metal finishes require special care to ensure that they remain in pristine condition. Everyday bathtub-cleaning chemicals are likely to damage surfaces, so follow manufacturers' guidelines.

SPECIALIZED TUB MATERIALS

Stainless steel, copper, marble, and wood can make exciting alternative materials for bathtubs but are expensive. Unlike acrylic or resin that are warm to the touch, materials such as stainless steel, copper, and marble are cold, absorbing heat from the water and reducing its temperature. Bathtubs can also be made from quality hardwoods. As well as being warm, they retain their heat well.

MAINTENANCE
Use a nonabrasive cleaner and soft cloth.

STAINLESS STEEL
Satin or mirror finishes are available.

△ **WOODEN BATHTUB**
Boards of solid hardwood are bonded together and protected with penetrating wood oil to provide a watertight seal. The moist conditions prevent the wood from drying out and so hold the boards together.

NATURAL WOOD
Clean lines and beautiful graining make a feature of this simple tub.

△ **STAINLESS STEEL BATH**
Stainless steel interiors are hygienic, durable, and easy to keep clean. The outer panel has been painted to give the illusion of solid veined marble.

SURFACE DETAIL
A roll top and deep sides show off the copper's gleam.

COPPER BATHTUB ▷
The distinctive vintage shape and copper interior have classic style. The copper is protected with a lacquer finish, but care must be taken not to scratch off the surface finish since blue-green staining can result.

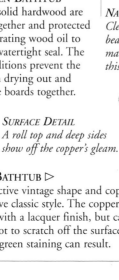

SHOWER SYSTEMS

A GOOD SHOWER IS UNBEATABLE, whether you prefer invigorating needle jets of water or a relaxing massage spray. A shower area can take up much less space than a bathtub and can be fitted into the smallest of rooms, making it ideal for small apartments and awkward areas. A variety of receptors, together with a huge choice of stalls and hardware, offer an infinite range of systems from which to choose.

SINGLE SHOWERS

A shower can be tailored to suit your exact requirements, from the shape and hardware to the temperature and speed at which water is delivered. Most showers are designed for one occupant with one shower head and one set of controls. Cubicle sizes vary, though, so it is worth stepping inside one to bend and stretch and check that you, and other members of your family, can shower in comfort.

▽ **CIRCULAR SHOWER**
An all-in-one shower unit can eliminate the need for additional plumbing, ceramic tiling, and electrical work. Here, an overhead spray, two pairs of body jets, integrated lighting, and storage for shampoos and soaps provide luxury in one compact unit.

BODY JETS
Jets of water massage shoulders and legs.

TEMPERATURE CONTROLS
A preselected temperature stays constant when showering.

SHOWER FINISH
Low-maintenance acrylic is durable and simple to wipe clean.

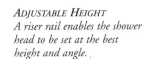

ADJUSTABLE HEIGHT
A riser rail enables the shower head to be set at the best height and angle.

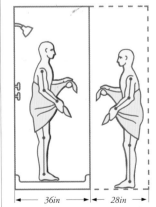

WASHING AND DRYING

— 36in — — 28in —

It should be possible to partly dry yourself within the confines of the shower unit. You will need space to raise your arms and to bend to reach your feet.

△ **STANDARD UNIT**
A standard square shower receptor will fit easily into the smallest of bathroom corners. A single shower head or combined shower head with body jets can be fitted to offer a range of showering options. Unless you choose a whole shower enclosure, a waterproof covering such as ceramic tiles must be used on the bathroom walls to prevent water penetration.

DOUBLE SHOWERS

For sharing a shower or for the luxury of having more room in which to move around, a double shower unit offers extra comfort. Most are rectangular, though round, square, and tapered designs offer flexibility when planning the layout.

▷ ▽ ANGLED SHOWER
The diagonally aligned shower door occupies the same area as a standard door; a roomy shower interior with multijet shower head, separate hand spray, and built-in seat showers one or two adults.

Doors have room to open even where space is limited.

WOODEN SEAT
A seat is useful for the less able as well as for those taking a long shower.

△ SHOWER ROOM
Fully tiled walls and a central drain for waste water open out a cramped room into a pleasant shower space. The large overhead shower head provides a deluge of water.

REMEMBER

■ Where space is limited, showers can be fitted under the stairs or on a landing.

■ Arrange quotes for the plumbing, tiling, and electrical work, and include these in your budget when working out the total price of the installation.

■ Check first with your installer that the system you intend to buy is compatible with your water supply.

■ Shower receptors come in five materials: steel, acrylic, resin, fiberglass, composite, and ceramic. Touch the surface to help make your choice.

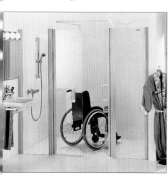

◁ SHOWERS FOR THE LESS ABLE
Watertight seals around the shower doors at floor level mean that less-abled users can move in and out of the shower enclosure without flooding the floor. A wide door and easily adjustable shower controls allow wheelchair access and privacy.

SHOWER SURROUNDS

Keeping the rest of the room dry and enjoying the benefits of an effective shower relies on containing the water within the showering space by means of a screen, door, or curtain. The least expensive option is a waterproof curtain, while the most expensive is a tempered glass surround.

△ SHOWER CURTAINS
PVC and plasticized fabrics used for modern shower curtains are impregnated with fungicide to prevent mildew.

SHOWER DOORS ▷
In the event of breakage, shower doors manufactured from tempered safety glass shatter like a car windshield into thousands of pieces that cause little harm.

△ STANDARD
Hinged on the left or right, the doors open into the bathroom.

△ INFOLD
Made in two sections, the door folds into the shower cubicle so that it does not take up any floor space.

△ PIVOT
Partly opening into the unit, the door occupies little space.

◁ ▽ SHOWER POD
Space and light are the main features of this spectacular shower room constructed from tempered frosted glass. Stainless steel handles are used to slide the doors open and closed. A wood floor and central shower head add to the pleasure of the experience.

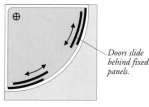

Doors slide behind fixed panels.

SHOWER AND TUB HARDWARE

GOOD-QUALITY HARDWARE is as important as the fixtures themselves. Many bathrooms are bought with hardware included in the price, but, as well as complementing the bathroom style, they should be durable and easy to operate – even with soapy hands. Shower, tub, and faucet hardware is used many times throughout the day, so invest time choosing the right details to ensure that even the most economical of bathrooms is a pleasure to use.

◁ **FIXED SHOWER**
A decorative swan-neck riser with a fixed shower head is ideal if you prefer a total soak rather than a light shower. The slender pipework remains static once in place, so you must supply a precise measurement for the shower height to ensure that you will be able to stand upright under the shower head.

FIXED HEAD
The jet of water cannot be adjusted.

BATH/SHOWER MIXERS

Bath/shower mixers are fitted with a diverter handle that can be switched over to fill the bathtub or to operate the shower. They are ideal for washing your hair and rinsing out the tub after use and are indispensable if there is no room in the house for a self-contained shower unit.

△ **RETRACTABLE HANDSET**
These telescopic hoses fit neatly within the tub surround and slide in and out for use. They are less likely to catch against any other hardware as the shower hose is put away. Not all bath/shower mixers are available with retractable handsets.

SHOWER CRADLE
The hand-held shower allows freedom of movement.

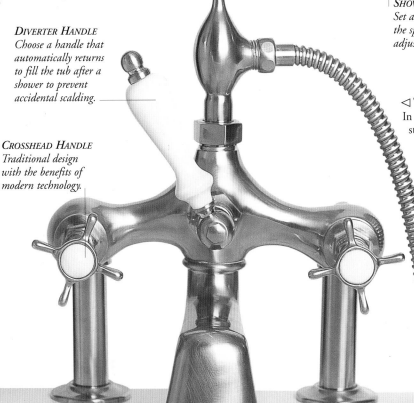

SHOWER HOSE
Flexible for a full-height shower or for rinsing the tub.

DIVERTER HANDLE
Choose a handle that automatically returns to fill the tub after a shower to prevent accidental scalding.

CROSSHEAD HANDLE
Traditional design with the benefits of modern technology.

SHOWER HEAD
Set at a fixed angle, the spray cannot be adjusted.

SHOWER SUPPLY
Try to buy all three elements of a fixed shower from the same supplier to ensure that they match.

◁ **TELEPHONE HANDSET**
In general, telephone handset designs fit standard bathtubs where three holes have been punched into the rim. However, some traditional handsets are available from specialized bathroom shops for nonstandard tubs and for tubs that have been recessed into a fixed surround, such as marble.

CERAMIC HANDLE
The diverter should move easily but feel secure when located in either the bath or shower position.

SHOWER HARDWARE

A shower must maintain a good flow of water at a constant temperature. Before purchase, check that the controls respond quickly and have built-in safety features to avoid scalding. Always check with the installer that the type of shower you want to purchase is compatible with your water supply.

◁ THERMOSTATIC CONTROL
Thermostatic shower controls are fitted with a shut-off valve to control the flow of water and maintain a constant temperature. The heat can be adjusted by mixing different volumes of hot and cold water.

HOSE
The pipe is reinforced to prevent buckling that will restrict water flow.

ELECTRICALLY HEATED ▷
An electric shower is connected to both the water and electricity supplies and heats water only when it is needed, making it very economical.

*SELF-CLEAN
By twisting the rim, small filaments push through the spray holes to eject scale.*

△ DIRECTIONAL HEAD
A fixed head is attached to the wall, and the pipework is hidden from view. The angle of the shower head can be altered to suit any user, while the spray options range from relaxing pulses to invigorating needle jets.

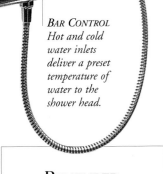

BAR CONTROL
Hot and cold water inlets deliver a preset temperature of water to the shower head.

REMEMBER

■ Single-control thermostatic faucets are easy to use by just turning the lever or dial from the off position through cold, warm, and then hot.

■ Dual-control thermostatic faucets regulate the water flow and keep the temperature constant. Antiscald devices are available that cut off over a hot but bearable 100°F/38°C.

■ Try out plumbed-in shower heads and faucets in bathroom showrooms to see how simple they are to operate.

■ When buying antique faucets and hardware, check that they will work with your fixtures.

BATHTUB HARDWARE

Many modern faucets have the latest ceramic disk technology, enabling them to be turned on or off fully with just a quarter turn. Ceramic disks have a hard, polished surface creating a watertight seal and drip-free "off" position. They also work well in hard water areas where scale can build up around faucets, making them difficult to operate.

△ RIM-MOUNTED FAUCETS
These are fitted to the edge of tubs that usually have pre-drilled tap-holes. All have a larger feed and flow capacity than sink faucets.

△ WALL-MOUNTED FAUCETS
Combined faucets and handles direct the flow of water. The faucets need to be sufficiently long to extend over the rim of the tub.

△ MOUNTED MIXER FAUCETS
Two handles and a central faucet are wall-mounted at the end of the tub or on one side. The plumbing is chaneled into the wall to hide it.

△ WATERFALL FAUCET
A wide band of water cascades into the bathtub and offers a neat, almost flush finish. Mixer handles keep an even water temperature.

WASTE

Dirty water from the tub, shower, bidet, and sink may drain out through the "waste," where a simple filter catches soap deposits and hair, which can then be removed periodically to prevent a blockage in the pipes. Wastes may be available from dealers specializing in vintage bathroom hardware.

△ POP-UP WASTE
Modern pop-up wastes are often operated from the faucet where a simple lever is lifted or depressed to open or seal the waste outlet. Their smooth surface is unobtrusive and comfortable if touched and cannot be accidentally pulled out when bathing.

*PLUG AND CHAIN
This system is still available and is often sold with a waste.*

SINK TYPES

MOST SINKS are supported on a pedestal or fitted within a countertop or washstand. These arrangements work well to conceal the plumbing, but the sink is set at a fixed height, which can be a disadvantage if you are taller or shorter than average. A wall-mounted sink, however, can be attached to the wall at a height that suits you.

PEDESTAL SINKS

Available in a huge variety of styles and sizes, pedestal sinks usually stand 34–36in (85–90cm) high. If you need even more height, you can raise the pedestal by standing it on a platform. Install the sink before mounting a backsplash to the wall behind to ensure that the sink will not interfere in the design.

INTEGRAL STORAGE ▷

The space beneath a sink is a useful place to hide toiletries that are not used on a day-to-day basis and to store bathroom cleaning equipment. As well as boxing in the pipework, a well-designed below-counter unit can become an interesting feature in its own right and contribute to the character of the bathroom. Open storage areas in bathrooms are best kept for attractive bath products and accessories (*see p.31 and pp.36–37*).

ASYMMETRIC SINK
The platform for resting a bar of soap adds both an element of interest and practicality to this freestanding design.

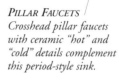

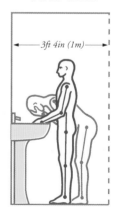

PILLAR FAUCETS
Crosshead pillar faucets with ceramic "hot" and "cold" details complement this period-style sink.

SWAN-NECK SPOUT
A high spout offers easy access to the washing bowl.

MIXER FAUCET
Hot and cold water temperature and flow can be mixed with precision.

OUTER EDGE
A high outside rim keeps the water within the sink.

SLIM PEDESTAL
A pedestal makes it easier to stand close to the sink.

△ STANDARD MODEL
Traditional ceramic pedestals are bolted to the floor and sometimes to the bathroom wall for stability. Pedestals provide additional support for the sink and hide any unsightly pipework.

COLOR DETAIL
A smooth ceramic sink, a gloss-painted pedestal, and a wooden storage unit make a durable and eye-catching arrangement.

STORAGE SPACE
The maple wood storage unit opens to reveal towels and other items.

TOE SPACE
Feet can be tucked under for closer access.

REMEMBER

■ Natural wood should be treated regularly with a coat of penetrating wood oil to repel water splashes and to maintain its distinctive graining. Warmth from bathroom radiators and heated towel bars can cause warping, so place wood items away from these elements.

■ Most manufacturers of bathroom ceramic fixtures offer a selection of countertop, wall-mounted or pedestal sinks, and the choice of smaller or larger than standard sink sizes.

■ Marble countertops can stain, so wipe up spills immediately, then buff with a soft cloth to avoid permanent damage.

SINK SIZE

←— 3ft 4in (1m) —→

Choose a sink that fits the space comfortably and leaves plenty of room to lean over and wash your face or brush your teeth without bumping into the wall behind.

WALL-MOUNTED SINKS

These space-saving sinks simply need mounting on a solid wall or upright that can take the weight of the sink when it is full of water. The waste outlet is hidden within a simple P-trap cover or a cylindrical "bottle-trap" (right). Free space beneath the sink makes the bathroom feel larger, and it can store bathroom weighing scales or a stool.

◁ **NEAT FIT**
The clever use of space means corner sinks can be tucked into the smallest of rooms. Choose faucets carefully; large ones will take up up too much of the wash area.

GLASS SINK ▷
A wall-mounted sink is simple to fasten to the wall at your own waist height for ease of use (*see also p.33*).

VANITIES AND WASHSTANDS

Traditional and modern washstands offer a range of facilities within one unit: sink, worktop, storage, shelving, and access to plumbing. The sink can be centered within the vanity with a countertop on either side, or placed off-center to provide a larger uninterrupted worktop for keeping makeup or shaving equipment close at hand.

△ **DOUBLE SINKS**
Twin sinks solve the problem of two people wanting to wash at the same time. A mirror running the length of the wall above the marble countertop and cupboards ensures that users do not get in each other's way.

WOODEN BAR
Towels can be draped over the bar, making a separate towel bar unnecessary.

ACCESS COVER
A removable plate means that plumbing is easy to reach in an emergency.

△ **WASHSTAND**
Natural wood, frosted glass, stainless steel, and wicker add interest and character to this open-fronted washstand. Simple accessories and white towels keep the look fresh and uncluttered, while semiopaque drawers mean that stored items are not forgotten and stay dust-free.

SHELF SPACE
An open shelf creates space for large and small items.

△ **VANITY**
Utilitarian items including toilet paper and cleaning materials are kept at hand but are hidden from view. The cupboards are fitted with adjustable shelves for extra flexibility.

SINK HARDWARE AND MATERIALS

THE CHOICE OF SINK MATERIAL can add an interesting new dimension to your overall bathroom design: many sinks are now made in a variety of shapes from specialized materials. When judging which hardware and surface finish best suit your needs, take into account your family's washing habits and how often the sink is used during the day.

DECK-MOUNTED FAUCETS

The ledge or rim of most sinks has pre-drilled holes that conform to a standard 1¼in (3.6cm) diameter. Whichever style of sink you choose, there is usually a one-hole, two-hole, or three-hole version to fit any faucet combination be it a single lever, a pair of pillars, or a three-piece sink mixer. When choosing, remember sink faucets are smaller than bathtub faucets.

COLOR CODED
Blue for cold and red for hot make handles easy to interpret.

△ **EASY-ACTION ATTACHMENTS**
Conventional handles require several turns to operate fully and can be difficult for the less able and children. Attachments such as these can be gripped and twisted more easily.

▽ **SINGLE-CONTROL FAUCET**
These faucets fit into a single hole, taking up much less sink space than two- or three-piece faucets. The main advantage of this design is the smooth, easy-to-operate lever that controls the flow and temperature of the water from the faucet.

HANDLE ACTION
A slim, "penlike" handle is simple to maneuver.

CHROME FINISH
A chromium-plated finish reflects other colors in the room.

△ **PILLAR FAUCETS**
Sink pillar faucets fit into a predrilled two-hole sink. These widely spaced faucets allow room to bring your head closer to the sink when washing your face or brushing your teeth.

△ **SINK MIXER**
Period-style ceramic handles operate the sink mixer to blend hot and cold water. The three-piece mixer set is designed for a three-hole sink.

WHITE CERAMIC
Simple lines and a smooth finish create a clean, crisp style.

SINGLE-CONTROL FAUCET
This delivers water at the desired temperature.

REMEMBER

Replacing old hardware can smarten up the look of your fixtures and may lessen the need for a brand-new bathroom suite.

Dark-colored and highly polished sink finishes should be kept in pristine condition or scratches, soap deposits, and scale will soon make them look tired.

Most waste systems require an area 12in (30cm) deep below the faucet for the mechanism to work. Bear this in mind if you intend to mount your sink in a countertop or washstand unit (*see pp.30–31*).

NATURAL FINISH

Wood may seem like an unusual choice of material for a sink, but the water-resistant properties of marine plywood make it a good choice if you prefer something a little different. The wood has been cleverly molded into shape by steam to form a sinuous line, then cut to provide a smooth ledge for storing sink accessories. A back panel protects the wall behind from splashes of water.

◁ SINGLE HANDLE

Like other sink mixer faucets, this simple design takes the guesswork out of running and mixing water to a comfortable temperature. The pipework is recessed so that the sink can be set closer to the wall.

▽ DOUBLE HANDLES

The distinctive "pepper mill" style handles have bulbous ends to help you grip and turn them even when wet. The position of the faucet is fixed so water falls into the sink.

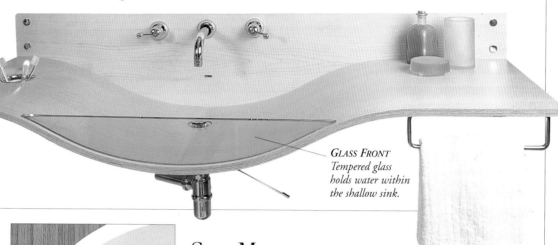
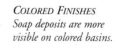

GLASS FRONT
Tempered glass holds water within the shallow sink.

POLISHED BRASS

prevent discoloration, solid brass highly polished and the surface ...ted with a protective finish that ...sts water and scratching. Non-...asive cleaners and buffing with ...ft cloth maintains the luster.

△ RECONSTITUTED MARBLE

Powdered marble is mixed with resin and colored to create a compound that feels as smooth as marble but is much stronger and stain-resistant. Numerous finishes can be chosen, from plain to veined marble effects.

SINK MATERIALS

Ceramic sinks are still the most popular choice, though the use of metal and glass designs is becoming more widespread. Marble, granite, wood, and mineral-resin compounds can be custom-made to suit specific requirements but are expensive. It is also worth noting that sinks set within a vanity or washstand must be well fitted with the sink edge sealed to prevent water from penetrating the surrounding unit. Deep inward-sloping rather than shallow sink rims will help protect the countertop area from stray splashes of water.

COLORED FINISHES
Soap deposits are more visible on colored basins.

CERAMIC ▷

Durable and very easy to clean, ceramic sinks are available in a range of colors to match any other fixture.

TEMPERED GLASS

...ck safety glass is durable and ...atch-resistant. It is shown off to best advantage when fixed on discreet brackets or a block of wood.

△ STAINLESS STEEL

Mirror-polished stainless steel looks good with contemporary chrome faucets. It wipes clean easily and is hygienic but the mirror finish can scratch, so opt for a brushed stainless steel finish for heavily used sinks.

TOILETS AND BIDETS

THE NEED FOR FRESHNESS, cleanliness, and hygiene dictates the most suitable materials for toilet and bidet manufacture, though the designs can be as aesthetically pleasing as other fixtures. The need for water conservation has been the driving force behind the latest designs, which combine style with environmentally friendly water-saving flush mechanisms.

VISIBLE TANKS

Most toilets have a tank that is both visible and easy to access in emergencies. The tank is usually placed flat against the wall, either above or directly behind the bowl. Elaborately ornate 19th-century tanks can be bought independently of the bowl but, on the whole, the tank is purchased as part of the toilet and includes the trip lever and flush mechanism.

EMBOSSED PANEL
A decorative panel hides ugly plumbing from view.

PULL CHAIN
Ceramic, wood, and metal handles can be chosen to match other fittings.

◁ **ONE-PIECE TOILET**
One-piece toilets have the tank and bowl attached, giving the most compact of all toilet designs. The tank rests on a ledge or platform at the back of the bowl and is also secured to the bathroom wall with sturdy mountings.

SLIMLINE TANK
A narrow tank allows the toilet bowl to be mounted up close to the wall so that it takes up no more space in the bathroom than is absolutely necessary.

SMOOTH EDGES
The seat follows the line of the bowl and does not overlap the edges.

HIGH-LEVEL TANKS ▷
If you wish to install this type of toilet, check that the ceiling is high enough; the tank needs to sit high above the bowl, connected by a pipe long enough to create enough force for a proper flush. High-level tanks can be noisy, but new technology has produced quieter models.

FLUSH PIPE
To look their best, chrome, brass, or gold-plated finishes should be mirror-polished.

REMEMBER

■ A high-level tank requires sturdy mountings to withstand the force applied to the flush and a strong wall to support the weight of the water in the tank when it is full.

■ Toilets with either high-level tanks or tall panel-style tanks will fit only on an uninterrupted wall space; otherwise, the flush pipe or tank height is likely to obstruct bathroom windows, molding, or cornicing.

■ Toilets and bidets need to be kept scrupulously clean, so choose models with smooth, curved lines that make all areas accessible. Select toilet seats with well-spaced hinges so that you can clean between the gaps.

■ The recommended position for using a standard height toilet is leaning forward with your feet tucked slightly back to emulate a squatting position.

GOOD POSTURE

Place the toilet so that there is head room.

The toilet bowl should be low enough for your feet to rest flat on the floor when sitting. There should also be headroom for a tall person to stand upright.

TOILETS WITH HIDDEN TANKS

Back-to-wall and wall-mounted toilets both use a tank that can be installed behind a false wall or paneling so that only the lever trip remains visible. Tanks are usually plastic and set at a minimum height of 32in (80cm).

BACK-TO-WALL TOILET ▷
With germ-harboring surfaces hidden away, back-to-wall designs are both hygienic and unobtrusive. Manufactured in brushed stainless steel, the bowl is easy to keep clean, while the adjacent floor and wall area can just be wiped over, making this a good choice for busy family bathrooms.

PRISTINE FINISH
Stainless steel is less likely to stain and take on odors.

◁ WALL-MOUNTED
Unlike back-to-wall types, wall-mounted designs sit above floor level. The weight of the toilet and the person sitting on it must be borne by the wall. Wall-mounted units work well in small bathrooms since they keep the floor area free and easy to clean.

COMFORT FACTOR
With wall-mounted designs, you can place the bowl at a height that suits you.

PERSONAL HYGIENE

Bidets are an invaluable aid to personal hygiene. Place them alongside the toilet so that they can be used after going to the toilet. They should be comfortable to sit on, so take care to choose a bidet with a curved rather than angular rim, and one that is wide enough to support both thighs and bottom.

BIDET MIXER
The directional nozzle also makes rinsing out the bidet much easier.

PEDESTAL BIDET ▷
Bidets mounted on pedestals are also useful for washing feet or the dirty hands and knees of young children. For this reason, it is practical to have towels close at hand and a nonslip floor surface where splashes can be quickly wiped up.

STRONG DETAIL
Select a bidet with a solid pedestal and a chunky outline for classic good looks.

◁ WALL-MOUNTED BIDET
Wall-mounted designs keep the bathroom floor clutter-free so that it can be kept scrupulously clean. The raised rim also prevents water from spilling onto the floor, while the colorful handles introduce a novel element to the functional.

TOILET SEATS

Seats come in many finishes, but standard hardware means that they can be fastened to most toilet bowls. Ideally, the seat should have a raised rim at the back, so that when you are seated the body is tilted forward into the squatting position.

LESS-ABLED SEAT
This specially designed seat raises the level of the rim so that it is easier to sit down.

◁ FAMILY SEAT
Smaller members of the family tend to slip through adult-sized seats. This flexible adapter has both a child seat and an adult seat. It also helps make child toilet training easier.

◁ POLISHED WOOD SEAT
A wooden seat is often more comfortable than plastic and feels warm. Here, carved-out "leg spaces" support the thighs.

JAZZY SEAT ▽
A new line of toilet seats made from colorful laminated plastics livens up the bathroom.

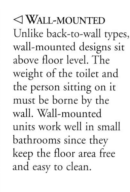

BOLD COLORS
Try a fun approach with amoeba shapes and vivid colors.

STORAGE

SPACE FOR STORING a range of products is often limited in bathrooms, but if it is well planned you can have shelves and open units to display attractive bottles and jars, plus areas behind closed doors for utilitarian items such as toilet tissue. Here, medicines can also be hidden from view, and out of reach of small children.

△ **OPEN-STORAGE TROLLEY**
A three-tiered trolley stores towels, toiletries, hair-grooming equipment, and cosmetics where they can be seen. It is easily moved to the activity area where the products are needed. Check that the trolley can glide across the floor and that the drawers do not stick.

FREESTANDING STORAGE

Bathroom cabinets and shelf units that stand alone take up valuable floor space, which can be a problem in small rooms. If this is the case, look for a cabinet that is raised above the floor so that items can be tucked underneath, or select a unit with glass shelves, which will look lighter.

STATIC STORAGE ▷
Take advantage of corner spaces, where fixtures will not fit, to place a tall storage unit. Towels, soaps, and accessories can be attractively displayed.

COMPARTMENT SPACE
Items kept within closed compartments are less susceptible to dust.

△ **CLOSED-STORAGE TROLLEY**
If you prefer closed storage, a trolley with closed units may be more useful so that bottles and jars of varying heights will be able to fit within the confines of the sections.

ADJUSTABLE HEIGHT
Shelf heights can be easily adjusted to suit the items you wish to display.

STORAGE HEIGHT

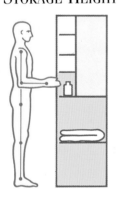

Items taken out frequently for use morning and night should be kept at the front of a wall cabinet, somewhere between waist height and eye level. Bulkier items, such as towels and cleaning equipment, are best kept on lower shelves.

WALL STORAGE

Apart from areas taken up by windows and doors, blank walls in small bathrooms present marvelous storage opportunities. Shelves and wall cabinets leave floor areas clear, and every item can be stored within arm's reach, just above or below eye level. Try to avoid deep shelves so that items do not become lost or forgotten at the back.

◁ **OPEN SHELVES**
Gradated shelf units – where the lowest shelf is shallowest – will not obstruct the bathroom occupant at shoulder height. Choose a style that is easy to keep clean and dust-free.

FROSTED GLASS
Less decorative items are hidden behind a semiopaque door but can be identified.

STREAMLINE SUPPORTS
Glass shelves and slimline brackets do not clutter up the limited wall space.

◁ **CUPBOARD STORAGE**
A mix of everyday items on display will clutter up countertops and look unsightly. Hide them from view by storing them in an attractive cabinet with a childproof safety lock.

REMEMBER

■ A bathroom can reveal a great deal about its owner. If you share it with others or visitors are likely to use it, keep your personal products hidden from view to avoid embarassing yourself or your visitors.

■ Mirrored cupboard fronts often have magnetic catches, making handles unnecessary. This leaves a clear, reflective area that gives the impression of additional light and space.

■ Piles of neatly folded towels look great in a bathroom, but they need to be kept fresh and aired or they may become damp and harbor mildew.

UNDERCOUNTER STORAGE

In compact bathrooms, built-in sinks and freestanding washstands with storage space beneath the sink area make good sense. Shelves should be easy to slide in and out so that you can adjust their height at will, since most toiletries, cosmetics, and toilet tissue vary enormously in size. It is also advisable to place very small items in containers so that they do not fall out every time you open the door. Access to plumbing under the sink is vital, since a leak in this storage area could ruin items such as cotton balls.

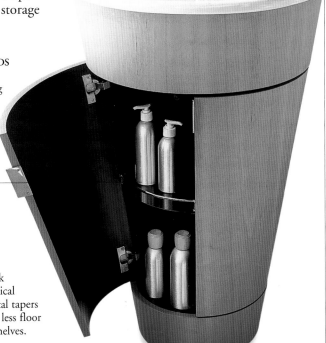

FAUCET FEATURE
A pop-up waste mechanism is mounted under the sink.

SINK DESIGN
A shallow sink sits neatly on top of the conical pedestal.

◁ **UNDERCOUNTER CUPBOARDS**
Melamine-faced units are easy to clean and can withstand bumping in bathrooms subject to heavy traffic. Use plastic containers to keep delicate items such as cotton balls dust-free.

BOTTLE SAFETY
A rail holds bottles in place and prevents them from falling out when the door is opened or closed.

PEDESTAL STORAGE ▷
A contemporary freestanding sink balances both aesthetic and practical needs. The conical-shaped pedestal tapers to the ground so that it occupies less floor space and is fitted with storage shelves.

HEATING AND VENTILATION

NOTHING DESTROYS THE PLEASURE of a glorious bath or shower more than stepping back into a cold room or drying yourself with damp towels. Wet skin is particularly sensitive to a drop in temperature, so heating and ventilation are important considerations when designing the room to make time spent in the bathroom, particularly during the colder winter months, an enjoyable part of your daily routine.

FREESTANDING HEATING

Radiators are the easiest and most widely used method of heating a bathroom because they are virtually maintenance-free. Other freestanding options – which look fabulous in traditional bathrooms – include coal-burning stoves and gas-fired fuel-effect designs. Both of these need insulation and proper ventilation.

BALL JOINTS
For a classic touch, choose high-polished finishes and ball joints.

△ **HEATED TOWEL RACK**
Useful for drying out and warming up towels, most heated racks should not be relied upon to heat the bathroom, too. Install a wall radiator as well for this purpose.

COLOR OPTIONS
Special heat-resistant paint finishes have been formulated for use on radiators.

METALLIC FINISHES
The rail is available in brass, chrome, and nickel finishes to match existing bathroom fixtures.

HEAT EFFECTIVE
Column radiators have a greater output than panel radiator designs.

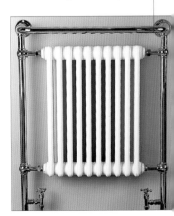

△ **RADIATOR TOWEL BAR**
If you have space for only one heater, choose a combination radiator that works in conjunction with your heating system and also has a bar for warming towels. Place the radiator so towels can be in easy reach of the bathtub or shower.

△ **COLUMN RADIATOR**
Most bathrooms are heated by radiators linked to the central hot-water system. Column radiators are effective heaters and work well in retro-style bathrooms. Alternatively, neat bathroom storage heaters can be installed to work on electricity.

AIR CIRCULATION
Leave space under and around the radiator to enable warm air to circulate.

SPACE-SAVING HEATING

It is surprising how much wall space a radiator or heated towel rack occupies – space that could well be used for an additional fixture or for storage. Several discreet, dual-purpose heaters are now on the market that will fit into the smallest of spaces. Some can be incorporated into the bathtub panel, while others fit into the kickspace under a storage unit.

△ WALL HEATER
A fan heater will provide warmth within moments of being switched on. Look for additional features, such as a choice of speed, heat settings, and a shaver socket.

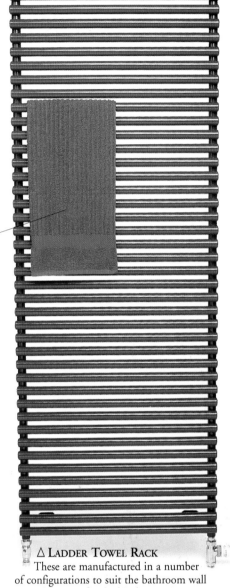

TOWEL SPACE
Make sure that the spaces between the bars can hold the largest of your towels.

◁ HEATED PANEL
Paneling around tubs is purely cosmetic, but some manufacturers produce a heated panel that will keep bath water warmer for a longer period, making bathing more enjoyable.

◁ PLINTH RADIATOR
Take advantage of "dead" space under bathroom units by installing a plinth radiator. The slim panel design is connected to the existing hot-water heating system, and it also works as a fan during the summer months. Booster settings will rapidly take the chill off a bathroom as the hot air rises from floor level to warm the room.

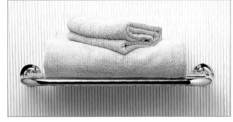

△ HEATED SHELF
Towels placed on the shelf are kept warm and aired with a heater element. Placed directly below a bathroom mirror, the heater element will also reduce misting and condensation.

△ LADDER TOWEL RACK
These are manufactured in a number of configurations to suit the bathroom wall space. They are finished in heat-resistant metallic or plain colors. Towels can be hung at a height that is practical for the user.

VENTILATION SYSTEMS

Good ventilation is required in bathrooms, because insulation and double glazing are so effective in modern homes that moisture-laden air does not disperse after a hot, steamy bath or shower. Instead, the moisture condenses on the walls, causing moisture and mold, as well as fabrics to mildew and wallpaper to peel.

△ HEAT RECOVERY
A heat exchanger saves 80 per-cent of heat that is expelled into the air with moisture; it transfers heat from warm out-going air to cold incoming air.

AIRFLOW IN A BATHROOM

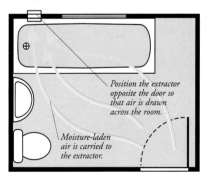

Position the extractor opposite the door so that air is drawn across the room.

Moisture-laden air is carried to the extractor.

Mounting an extractor fan to the outside wall is a simple way to expel air quickly from the room and reduce steam and condensation; ducting is a more complicated alternative.

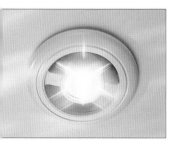

◁ LIGHT EXTRACTOR
A buildup of steam in a shower cubicle tends to block out the light. To overcome this problem, install a low-voltage ceiling light in the shower unit. Choose a system that has a built-in extractor fan to draw away the steam.

LIGHT SOURCES

WELL-CONSIDERED LIGHTING and your choice of window treatment will contribute enormously to the character of the bathroom. Consider accent lighting to highlight key areas, mood lighting for a soothing atmosphere, or bright, functional lighting for a family room, but bear in mind that water and electricity are a lethal mix, so the fixtures you select must be safe. Your choice of window treatment has no such limits but should provide both privacy and style.

PLANNED LIGHTING SYSTEM
Diffused lighting casts a soft background illumination; accent lighting focuses on the sinks.

POINTS TO CONSIDER

■ Safety features are of paramount importance when selecting lighting for bathrooms. Ensure ceiling lights are sealed within a glass or plastic steam-proof diffuser. Waterproof bulkhead lights – designed for garden use – work well in bathrooms, particularly showers, where the shower doors reduce the light level. Even though bulkheads are waterproof, always mount them high on the wall or overhead where they cannot be accidentally knocked or drenched by water from the shower head.

■ Fluorescent lighting gives a clear, shadowless light but can look cold and harsh in bathrooms. Reduce the glare by placing fluorescent tubes behind a diffuser panel. Bathroom cabinets are often fitted with fluorescent lights to throw light onto the countertop below.

■ Good lighting will make it easier to perform intricate bathroom activities, such as applying cosmetics and shaving. It can also highlight hazardous wet areas on the floor where you could slip.

■ For safety, bathroom lights may be switched on and off by a pull cord inside the bathroom or by a switch outside the room to prevent water from coming into contact with the electrical wiring.

(sidebar, rotated) **WINDOW TREATMENTS** **LIGHTING**

OPAQUE GLASS

This glass can be plain or have a textured, acid-etched, or sandblasted finish to echo the bathroom theme.

ADVANTAGES
• Obscures the view from passersby.
• Makes curtains or blinds unnecessary.
• Allows maximum daylight to filter through.

DISADVANTAGES
• Hand-finished designs can be expensive.
• Can look cold and clinical.
• Does not retain heat in winter.

OVERALL LIGHTING

A central light or several downlighters will cast an even light over the whole room but can lack imagination and may be unsuitable for task areas.

ADVANTAGES
• Simple to plan and install.
• Casts an even light over the room.
• Wide choice of styles and fixtures available.

DISADVANTAGES
• Uniform lighting is not always interesting.
• Shows up imperfection on walls and ceilings.
• Angles difficult to adjust.

ROLLER BLINDS

Offering a vast choice of colors, patterns, and textures, roller blinds draw attention to the window area.

ADVANTAGES
Easy to mount.
Take up a minimum amount of space.
Huge choice of colors and designs.

DISADVANTAGES
Block out light if you want daytime privacy.
Difficult to clean and dust.
Some spring mechanisms can jam in use.

CURTAINS

Adding interest and color, curtains emphasize your taste and style, and they frame an otherwise plain window.

ADVANTAGES
• Can coordinate with the color scheme.
• Make bathrooms look less cold and clinical.
• Retain heat within the room.

DISADVANTAGES
• Dust and steam can damage the fabric.
• Opening and closing can be disruptive.
• Can be expensive.

SHUTTERS

Slatted shutters maintain privacy without blocking out the natural light. Their simple style works well in bathrooms.

ADVANTAGES
• Slats can be angled to let in daylight.
• Can be finished in natural wood or colors.
• Take up little space.

DISADVANTAGES
• Are usually custom-made and expensive.
• Slats can be difficult to clean.
• Humidity may cause wood to expand.

DIFFUSED LIGHTING

Nondirectional lighting offers a soft, ambient atmosphere that is successful in both hi-tech and traditional bathrooms where a relaxed environment is desired.

ADVANTAGES
Has a relaxing effect.
Can disguise less than perfect surfaces.
Reduces glare from mirrors and white fixtures.

DISADVANTAGES
Cannot be used for task lighting.
Can be expensive.
May need additional light sources.

TASK LIGHTING

Bathroom activities performed in front of a mirror, such as putting in contact lenses, need task lighting to provide a direct, clear source of light.

ADVANTAGES
• Can be directed where required.
• Boosts light in otherwise gloomy areas.
• Can be wall- or ceiling-mounted.

DISADVANTAGES
• May bounce off white surfaces, causing glare.
• Provides an unflattering light for complexions.
• Throws strong shadows.

AMBIENT LIGHTING

A soft light transforms a bathroom by creating a warm and tranquil setting in which to relax. Candlelight is the most atmospheric with its flickering glow.

ADVANTAGES
• Disguises surface blemishes.
• Offers a soft, all-around calming light.
• Makes bathing and showering an event.

DISADVANTAGES
• Several candles are needed to cast enough light.
• Cheap candles can produce plumes of smoke.
• Candles must be set away from fabrics for safety.

FLOORING

STEAM, SPLASHES, WET FOOTPRINTS, and spilled creams and lotions all take their toll on bathroom flooring, so choosing a suitable material needs careful thought. Before coming to a decision, consider each flooring material in terms of durability, comfort, hygiene, and aesthetic appeal. Carpets, for example, are soft and comfortable to walk on with bare feet but can rot in damp conditions, while ceramic tiles are durable but cold underfoot. Weigh up the pros and cons of each to avoid a costly mistake.

HAND-COLORED TILES
A highly imaginative use of color turns a patchwork of tiles into a kaleidoscope of tones.

MARBLE

Marble flooring has a timeless quality, making it a desirable choice for both contemporary and traditional bathrooms

ADVANTAGES
• Durable and easy to maintain.
• Natural beauty does not deteriorate with age.
• Smooth surface will not harbor dust or dirt.

DISADVANTAGES
• Slippery when wet and may stain.
• Expensive to buy and lay.
• Requires a sturdy subfloor below.

LINOLEUM

A natural material that presents some of the most versatile options in creative flooring. Custom-made floor patterns are designed with the aid of a compute

ADVANTAGES
• Extremely durable.
• Good for allergy sufferers; it will not hold dus
• Warm and quiet underfoot.

DISADVANTAGES
• More expensive than most vinyl flooring.
• Must be laid by an experienced fitter.
• Can crack if the subfloor is not level.

POINTS TO CONSIDER

■ No matter how good the flooring you choose, incorrect fitting or laying will result in an uneven surface that will wear badly. Always have the flooring installed by a professional fitter; most guarantees will be invalidated if the material is laid incorrectly.

■ Unless laid by an expert, the weight of ceramic, stone, and marble flooring can cause a weak suspended wood floor to sag. As wood expands and contracts with changes in warmth and humidity, tiles may crack or grout fracture. So a plywood layer is fitted before the tiles are laid to ensure that the flooring remains stable.

■ Strong detergents and abrasive cleaners can ruin highly polished or vinyl floor coverings, producing discoloration on pale surfaces and the appearance of matte patches. Always check the manufacturer's instructions for the best method of cleaning.

■ Bear in mind that busy or large floor patterns may overpower the rest of the bathroom, especially if the room is small and the fixtures are plain.

■ Natural coir matting is well suited to bathrooms since the fibers benefit from being kept moist, but it can be prickly on bare feet.

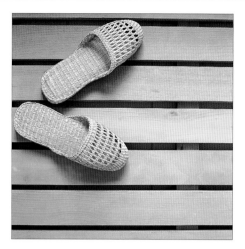

CERAMIC TILES

Durable and impermeable, these tiles can take a good deal of punishment and are available in a wealth of colors.

ADVANTAGES
Low-maintenance and almost indestructible.
Widely available and relatively inexpensive.
Produced in neutral, pastel, and primary hues.

DISADVANTAGES
Slippery when wet, and cold underfoot.
Noisy when walked on in shoes.
Grouting can be difficult to clean.

LIMESTONE

Along with other natural stones, pale gray limestone has a characteristic grain and texture that improves with age.

ADVANTAGES
• Natural color blends with all bathroom styles.
• Easy-to-clean surface.
• Extremely durable.

DISADVANTAGES
• Expensive to buy and install.
• Cold to walk on barefoot.
• Slippery when wet.

WOOD

The color, grain, and warmth of wood make it a popular choice in all rooms, but bathroom floors must be sealed.

ADVANTAGES
• Many kinds are simple to install.
• Mellows and improves with age.
• Works well in modern and traditional settings.

DISADVANTAGES
• Needs regular maintenance to look its best.
• Water penetration can swell and lift boards.
• Noisy when walked on in shoes.

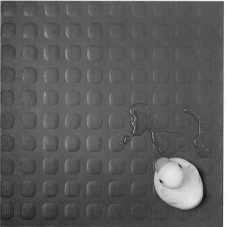

VINYL

The most inexpensive and widely used type of floor covering, produced in both sheet and tile form. Designs range from plain finishes to textured marble.

ADVANTAGES
Inexpensive and easy to lay.
Warm, soft, and quiet underfoot.
Durable and waterproof.

DISADVANTAGES
Ripples appear if laid on an uneven surface.
Discolors if exposed to sunlight.
Damaged by heavy furniture or shoe heels.

RUBBER

Stud rubber flooring is available in sheet or tile form. It is both durable and water-resistant; many architects choose it for commercial buildings.

ADVANTAGES
• Virtually indestructible.
• Quiet and warm to walk on.
• Waterproof surface has antislip finish.

DISADVANTAGES
• Expensive to buy.
• Stocked only by speciality floor suppliers.
• Must be installed by an experienced fitter.

CARPET

Probably the most popular floor covering, it offers comfort and warmth, and it also prevents noise from an upstairs bathroom reaching downstairs.

ADVANTAGES
• Available in sheet or tile form.
• Vast range of colors, patterns, and piles.
• Prices to suit all budgets.

DISADVANTAGES
• Steam and water cause some backings to rot.
• Requires regular vacuuming to maintain look.
• Padding must be laid to give good wear.

WALLCOVERINGS

THE MATERIALS YOU CHOOSE to furnish the walls in bathrooms can vary from zone to zone. Shower and bathtub areas take the greatest punishment, so wallcoverings chosen for these "wet" areas must be able to stand up to frequent soaking and be easy to wipe clean. For other more general areas of the bathroom, paint or wallpapered finishes may be more appropriate, but even these wallcoverings must have a washable finish and be specially treated to restrict mildew in the humid bathroom environment.

PAINT

Specially formulated bathroom paints have a washable vinyl finish. They also contain fungicides to restrict mildew.

ADVANTAGES
• Inexpensive to buy.
• Quick and easy to apply.
• Infinite range of colors available.

DISADVANTAGES
• Paint will mark, so backsplashes are needed.
• Looks dull if used on large expanses of wall.
• Not tough enough to be used in shower areas.

HARDWORKING WALLS
Architectural glass bricks allow light to penetrate, while mosaic tiles are durable and easy to clean.

CERAMIC TILES

A wide range of tile colors, patterns, and sizes are produced that are suitable for all bathroom areas including the shower surround.

ADVANTAGES
• Easy-to-clean.
• Heat-resistant and waterproof.
• Reasonably priced.

DISADVANTAGES
• Must be laid on sound walls or may crack.
• Square tiles can look monotonous in large areas.
• Grouting can attract dirt and mildew.

POINTS TO CONSIDER

■ Exterior bathroom walls are colder and so more prone to condensation. Select an insulating wallcovering, such as a vinyl or a paint specially formulated for bathrooms or kitchens, to reduce the problem.

■ High walls can make a small bathroom appear cold and clinical. Balance the proportions of the room by selecting one color for lower walls and a coordinating color for the upper walls. Molded tiles mounted at picture-rail height can create an effective horizontal break in a large area of wall, as can wood moldings that have been stained or painted.

■ Pale colors make bathrooms appear lighter and more spacious. Choose large mirrors placed opposite natural light sources to give the impression of additional space.

■ Paint is the most versatile and inexpensive of wallcoverings and offers the opportunity to experiment with a wide range of finishes from sponging to stenciling. The effects and colors can be selected to achieve total coordination.

■ Look for a wallcovering that features a complementary color in its design or opt for one that contrasts with the fixtures you have chosen to install in the bathroom.

WALLPAPER

Vinyl finishes are best for bathrooms, last longer, and give a bathroom a more furnished, comfortable appearance.

ADVANTAGES
- Readily available and inexpensive.
- Easy to hang.
- Wide range of colors, patterns, and finishes.

DISADVANTAGES
- Can hide fungal growth behind the paper.
- May peel or bubble in humid conditions.
- Thin paper may show up wall imperfections.

TEXTURED PLASTER

Rough plaster is a fashionable finish, but it must be sealed in bathrooms to prevent water from penetrating.

ADVANTAGES
- Masks uneven wall surfaces.
- Requires no special skills to apply.
- Is a durable and inexpensive finish.

DISADVANTAGES
- Rough plaster attracts dust and dirt.
- Can scratch bare skin.
- Cannot be used in shower area.

WOOD PANELING

Useful for boxing in a tub and covering up uneven walls, wood paneling must be sealed to make it water-resistant.

ADVANTAGES
- Easy to install, even for the amateur.
- Inexpensive and widely available.
- Can be painted or stained to your specification.

DISADVANTAGES
- Cheaper softwood panels can dent if hit hard.
- Moisture may cause the wood to warp.
- May not suit all styles of bathroom.

MOSAIC

Available in sheet form for ease of use, mosaic tiles are extremely durable and water-resistant, making them ideal for shower enclosures and backsplashes.

ADVANTAGES
- Adds character and interest to all surfaces.
- Generally easy to lay.
- Offers interesting design opportunities.

DISADVANTAGES
- Intricate designs are time-consuming.
- Grout can harbor soap and dirt.
- Can look industrial if used over large areas.

GLASS BRICKS

Ideal as a screen where natural daylight needs to be "borrowed" from another living area, glass bricks look best in contemporary spaces.

ADVANTAGES
- Add an area of interest.
- Are extremely durable and waterproof.
- Allow light to filter through.

DISADVANTAGES
- Expensive.
- Need to be installed professionally.
- Can make a bathroom appear cold.

GRANITE

A natural stone, granite comes in a range of tones. It is ideal for backsplashes and is best kept to small areas, especially dark stone, which can look hard and cold.

ADVANTAGES
- Durable and easy to maintain.
- Easy to clean.
- Can enhance the simplest bathroom.

DISADVANTAGES
- Expensive.
- Requires expert installation.
- Can be cold against the skin.

ROOM PLANS

FITTED BATHROOM PLAN

ALL BATHROOMS BENEFIT from good planning because key fixtures must be fitted into a limited area without the user feeling cramped. A fitted design capitalizes on all available space from floor to ceiling. All plumbing and ducting is boxed in, and slim storage units are shoehorned into narrow spaces. Mosaic and melamine offer durable finishes in bold colors and present simple, clutter-free surfaces in both wet and dry areas.

SLIM UNIT
A fitted cupboard set between the windows at eye level stores soaps, shower gels, and shampoos close to the tub.

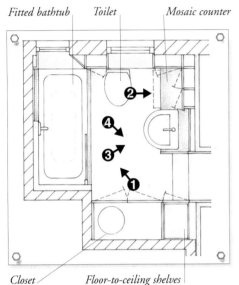

Fitted bathtub   Toilet   Mosaic counter

INTERNAL ROOM DIMENSIONS:
7ft 8in (2.4m) wide
8ft 8in (2.7m) long

Closet   Floor-to-ceiling shelves

△ BIRD'S-EYE VIEW
Windows above the tub and toilet filter daylight into the room. The toilet is against the outside wall for access to the vent pipe. Other items are built in to not obstruct movement in the room.

OPTICAL ILLUSION
A wide, sloping sill balances the small window frame with the larger one next to it.

FIXTURES
A white tub, toilet, and sink look clean and simple within this bold color scheme.

AWKWARD RECESS
A recess, too narrow for shelves, is put to good use with a large, light-reflecting mirror.

△ ❶ BATHTUB SURROUND
The back wall is just long enough for a full-sized tub to be fitted flush against it. Dazzling blue mosaic tiles provide a durable, waterproof surface for the back wall and tub edge, while a mirror fitted into the recess reflects light from the window, keeping the area bright and open.

FOR MORE DETAILS...

Wall-mounted toilet SEE P.35

Wall storage SEE P.37

Opaque glass SEE P.40

Mosaic tiles SEE P.45

BATHTUB SURROUND
Mosaic provides a waterproof ledge on which to place washing items.

❷ SMALL DIVISIONS ▷
Most bathroom products are packaged in small containers and tubes, so individual cupboards divided up by shelves keep them neat, easy to find, and less likely to become lost or forgotten.

DISCREET CUPBOARDS
Personal items and medicines are hidden behind push-open panels without handles.

SINK HEIGHT
A half-countertop sink is set into the surface so that the sink sits at a suitable height.

FLOOR-TO-CEILING STORAGE
A slim unit with adjustable shelf heights stores bathroom towels and toilet tissue.

△ ❸ SPACE SOLUTIONS
The sink is offset to the right of the fitted units to provide a large area of mosaic worktop to the left on which to place items in use. The orange paneling beneath the sink neatly conceals the plumbing and has space for storing essential bathroom cleaning materials. To the left of the sink, a large wooden hamper slides open to collect dirty laundry. Like the rest of the cupboards, there is no handle on the hamper to interrupt the simple, fitted look; instead, it opens by placing your finger into the cut-out finger hole. The mirror above the sink magnifies the whole bathroom, making it appear much larger than it actually is.

NONSLIP STAIRS
Steps leading down to the bathroom are trimmed with a nonslip edge to prevent accidents.

CLOSET
Decorative holes in the plywood doors allow air to circulate around the hot-water tank inside.

DESIGN POINTS

■ Strong blocks of color work best where there is plenty of natural daylight to maintain a fresh, spacious environment.

■ Marine plywood can be used throughout bathrooms since it is water-resistant. Alternatively, use standard plywood and coat the natural wood finish in yacht varnish; this will protect it from water splashes and humidity, which can cause the wood to warp.

■ Wall-mounted toilets and bidets require paneling to hide away the plumbing mechanics of each item. This often creates storage space within the boxed-in area, and a top edge that serves as a useful shelf for bathroom accessories.

△ ❹ PRACTICAL MATERIALS
All the surfaces have been constructed out of materials that suit bathroom conditions, are inexpensive, and are readily available: water-resistant paint finishes for the front of the units and window frames, plywood for the cupboard, and mosaic. The result is an interesting and original, fully fitted bathroom.

FITTED BATHROOM IDEAS

△ WALL-TO-WALL VENEER
A rich oak veneer covers the walls, cupboards, and drawers to produce a uniform effect that ensures the back-to-wall toilet panel and varying-height units blend unobtrusively. Sets of drawers contain toiletries and accessories, leaving surfaces clear for decorative items. Areas that could become wet or marked are finished in marble, which is both practical and attractive.

△ FITTED HEATING
Primrose-yellow paneling is chosen throughout the bathroom to make it appear brighter and larger. Fitted units and open shelves make good use of space below the sink, and a panel heater in the kickspace makes a wall radiator unnecessary.

◁ LESS IS MORE
Simple chrome hardware ensures that the beauty of the natural wood and marble can be fully appreciated. The two sink recesses, cut out of a marble worktop, echo the straight lines and symmetry of the wall cupboards. Diffused lighting reflects in the wall-to-wall mirror.

MARBLE SIMPLICITY ▷
A single sheet of pale gray marble is fitted along the length of the left wall, with a sink set to one end to maximize the countertop area. The same finish is applied to the end wall and the bath surround, creating continuity as well as an attractive hardwearing surface; spills must be wiped up or marble may stain.

UNFITTED BATHROOM PLAN

UNLIKE FITTED BATHROOMS, where cabinets fill every space from floor to ceiling, the unfitted plan takes a more relaxed approach. Here, furnishing the bathroom like a boudoir, with a comfortable armchair and other pieces of furniture not usually associated with bathroom design, is encouraged. With a large bathtub as the focus, this room is a special place in which to unwind.

Armchair　*Roll-top bathtub*　*Toilet*

INTERNAL ROOM DIMENSIONS:
10ft 4in (3.2m) wide
11ft 4in (3.5m) long

Fireplace

Linoleum floor　*Double doors*　*Pedestal sink*

△ BIRD'S-EYE VIEW
The tub sits in the middle of the room in front of a cast-iron fireplace. An alcove to the left of the fireplace houses a close-coupled toilet; the alcove on the right has a pedestal sink.

△ ❶ ROLL-TOP BATHTUB
A beautiful piece of furniture in its own right, an antique roll-top tub can be placed at any angle in the room, because the plumbing is concealed within metal shrouds that rise up from the floor. This bathtub has been positioned in front of the fireplace and makes a wonderfully bold focal point.

WINDOW TREATMENT
A plain roller blind softened by drapes provides warmth, style, and privacy.

ARMCHAIR
A big comfortable chair provides a place to relax following a luxurious bath.

CHEST OF DRAWERS
Towels and toiletries are stored in deep drawers, while cosmetics, brushes, and a mirror sit on top.

FIREPLACE
The coal-burning fire creates a cozy, intimate atmosphere when lit.

ANTIQUE DETAIL
A mahogany wall shelf adds to the "furnished" look of the room.

DESIGN POINTS

■ Unfitted bathroom designs also work with contemporary fixtures and furniture.

■ Exploit architectural features, such as alcoves and a fireplace to add extra character to the room.

■ Details, such as pictures, fresh flowers, and candles, contribute to the "furnished" look.

■ Polish wooden furniture to protect it from humidity and water splashes which eventually cause wood to warp.

SHELF UNIT
A brass gallery shelf displays a selection of bottles and jars.

△ ❷ PERIOD STYLE
The alcove to the right of the fireplace is large enough to accommodate a full-sized pedestal sink with "elbow room" and adequate wall space above for a shelf and cabinet. Brass faucets and other hardware have been chosen to reinforce the period theme. The deep ochre walls create a warm backdrop for the white fixtures and the pale fireplace area and also show off the mahogany pieces of furniture to best advantage.

△ ❸ BATHING ATMOSPHERE
The importance of lighting for setting the atmosphere in a room is often underestimated. Here, the roll-top bathtub and other pieces of furniture are lit by the warm glow of the candlelight and firelight, which create a soothing environment for bathing. For some, candlelight may seem an impractical choice. Low-voltage halogen downlights operated from a dimmer switch (outside of the room) may offer a more practical solution. Halogen downlights are both neat and unobtrusive, and will cast a bright light for everyday tasks.

FOR MORE DETAILS...

Freestanding tub SEE P.22

Pedestal sink SEE P.30

Linoleum flooring SEE P.42

Roller blinds SEE P.44

FLOOR DETAIL
Cut to resemble a period tiled floor, linoleum provides warmth underfoot.

UNFITTED BATHROOM IDEAS

△ CLEAN LINES
Diagonally placed fixtures offer an interesting alternative layout. The tub's position contrasts with the horizontal lines of the windows and doors in the adjacent room, while the monochromatic color scheme creates a strong visual link and gives a sharp, clean-cut look to this stylish bathroom.

△ SET PIECE
A large limed-oak linen press with paneled doors and raised cornice is the focal point of this traditional bathroom. The press is placed on a wall opposite the tub, so that the fresh towels and toiletries are nearby. The freestanding clothes valet, washstand, and large oval mirror create an air of elegance.

◁ CLASSIC COMFORT
Dark wood and antique furniture turn this bathroom into an informal, comfortable room that blends easily with the classic fixtures and flooring. A weeping fig tree in the corner has architectural proportions and creates a screen between the bathroom and the bedroom when the adjoining doors are both open.

FUN AND FUNCTION ▷
Acres of space in this warehouse apartment allow an adventurous layout. There are no hard partitions or walled-in wash areas to inhibit movement. When privacy is needed, an area can be divided off with a striped screen. Two stainless steel sinks and a clever division of space mean that more than one person can use the room.

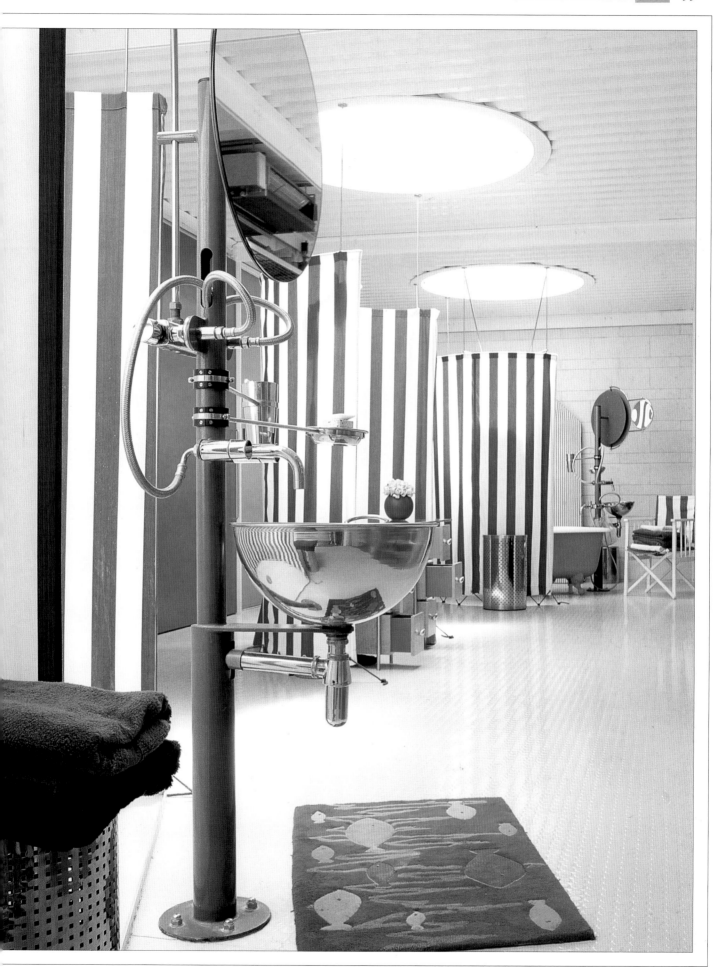

IMPROVISED BATHROOM PLAN

EVEN WITH LIMITED FUNDS, it is possible to apply the ergonomic principles of bathroom design and produce excellent results. Rather than pulling out your existing fixtures and starting from scratch, assess what you like and dislike about the bathroom. Perhaps by just changing the lighting or bathtub and sink hardware you can create a space that is a pleasure to use.

Low-level toilet   Fitted tub

OPAQUE GLASS
Inexpensive to fit, opaque glass offers privacy and a modern finish.

◁ **BIRD'S-EYE VIEW**
This narrow bathroom contains a rectangular bathtub, pedestal sink, and toilet, with enough space between each item to use them comfortably. It benefits from a large window on the end wall that lets in natural light.

Sink

Hamper

INTERNAL ROOM
DIMENSIONS:
4ft 9in (1.5m) wide
10ft 1in (3.1m) long

LOW-LEVEL TOILET
The original low-level toilet remains against the wall. The pipes have been repainted to give them a fresher look.

△ ❶ **WORKING SPACE**
If existing fixtures are in good condition, there is no need to change them. Replacing small details, such as the seal around the bathtub, and renewing or whitening tile grouting can make all the difference, giving a room a new lease on life.

FOR MORE DETAILS...

Sink hardware SEE P.32
Overall lighting SEE P.40
Linoleum SEE P.42
Ceramic tiles SEE P.44

LINOLEUM TILES
New buff-colored tiles are laid on a hardboard base; they must be glued down well or water may cause them to lift.

PAINT FINISH
Specially formulated bathroom paint is inexpensive and reduces the chance of condensation and mildew.

MIRRORED CABINET
A cabinet that doubles up as a mirror offers a budget solution to storing products used on a daily basis.

DESIGN POINTS

■ Unless the plan of the bathroom can be improved, leave the fixtures where they are; removing them could cause unnecessary expense.

■ Updating the tub and sink hardware alone can transform the look of fixtures at a fraction of the price of a complete refit.

■ New white grouting can improve the look of old tiles.

■ New blinds and curtains divert attention from a dull view.

△ ❷ NEW TECHNOLOGY
Old faucets and hardware lose their mirror brightness over time, and scale builds up on the surface, making them look permanently dirty. Holes are predrilled to a standard size, so it is simple to replace the old tub and sink faucets with new hi-tech ones (*see p.29*). Plugs and chains can also be changed.

WALL TILES
Half-tiled walls provide a durable waterproof surface where needed.

△ ❸ IDEAS IN ACTION
A central ceiling light has been removed to make way for chrome halogen downlights, which are low-voltage and operated by a pull-cord, so they are safe to use in bathrooms. Arranged in pairs, the lights accentuate areas over the tub, toilet, sink, and doorway. A mirror-fronted cabinet and mirror on the opposite wall also help bounce light around the room. As an inexpensive alternative to a combined radiator towel bar (*see p.38*), a chrome bar has been mounted over the radiator to warm towels as the room is being heated.

HAMPER
A wooden hamper adds style and can also double as a bathroom stool.

IMPROVISED BATHROOM IDEAS

△ BRIGHT DESIGN

When plain white tiles that are inexpensive and widely available are teamed up with brightly colored ceramics, paint, and towels, the effect is fun and upbeat. The old cabinet doors have been replaced with fabric to match the ceramics.

STENCILED STARS ▷

If it is not within your budget to change the design of your bathroom to suit your needs, transform its appearance by stenciling the walls, floor, and ceiling. On a larger budget a new bathroom floor and lighting can make a huge difference.

◁ MEDITERRANEAN UPDATE

Painting the bathroom is one of the least expensive ways to instantly improve its appearance. Here, deep blue and seafoam colors make a focal point of the white tub, while a beachcomber's hoard of stones and pebbles, arranged under the tub, create an artistic finishing touch.

▽ FRESH APPROACH

Keep existing fixtures; finish the bathroom walls in tongue-and-groove paneling painted white. A budget wallcovering, it helps to conceal uneven walls and ceilings. A new toilet seat and faucets help update old fixtures.

△ OLD FASHIONED MATERIALS

One way to improve a large bathroom on a restricted budget is to buy fixtures and hardware from an architectural salvage yard. Although supplies are not guaranteed, a hand-decorated toilet, roll-top tub, and hardware can be bought for less than the cost of modern reproductions.

DUAL-PURPOSE BATHROOM PLAN

A LARGE, LUXURIOUS BATHROOM where space is given over to activities other than bathing can make good planning sense. Obvious partnerships include a bathroom-cum-dressing room where you can wash, dress, and groom yourself in privacy, or a bathroom and fitness room where you can shower after exercising and take a sauna.

Roll-top tub   *Wardrobes*   *Dressing table*   *Shelves*

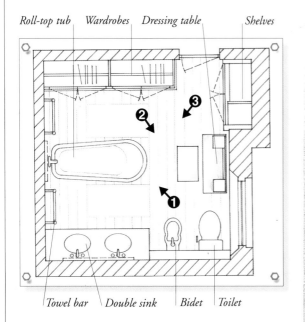

Towel bar   *Double sink*   *Bidet*   *Toilet*

△ BIRD'S-EYE VIEW
The bathtub sits in the center of the room well away from the fitted wardrobes, shelves, sinks, dressing table, toilet, and bidet. All the facilities are well-spaced around the large room so that a sense of order prevails.

INTERNAL ROOM
DIMENSIONS:
11ft 4in (3.5m) wide
11ft 7in (3.6m) long

HANGING SPACE
Clothes are hung up, while hats and shoes are stacked on shelves above and below.

PANELED DOORS
The lower section of the doors are paneled to match the other walls.

METAL SHROUDS
Chrome-plated cylinders cover the pipework.

◁ ❶ SURFACE DETAIL
All the surfaces – wall paneling, door fronts, and floorboards – are painted in the same low-sheen paint finish so that they are both durable and waterproof. The wardrobe doors are paneled to look like the walls and are fitted with self-closing magnetic catches so that they are unobtrusive when closed.

STORAGE
Shelves beneath the double sink store toiletries and cosmetics.

❷ DUCTED PLUMBING ▷
The lower section of the walls around the bathroom are clad in tongue-and-groove paneling. Behind the toilet and bidet the wood panels are brought forward to box in the maze of pipework required to use the toilet and bidet.

NATURAL LIGHT
The dressing table and mirror are situated close to the window to benefit from natural light.

DRESSING TABLE
Small drawers next to the mirror store cosmetics and beauty products close at hand.

CENTRAL HEATING
A large room such as this needs to be well-heated. A grille provides an attractive and safe cover for the large radiator.

WALL SPACE
Lining up a low-level toilet, bidet, and sink leaves wall space above for a mirror and painting.

DESIGN POINTS

■ Leave access points in the paneling where pipework can be easily reached for any essential maintenance.

■ Painted floors can be slippery when wet, so choose a suitable low-sheen finish and provide cotton mats with nonslip backings to absorb splashes.

■ When a bathtub sits in the middle of a room, supply a tub rack for soap and sponge.

❸ LIGHT AND SPACE ▷
Every activity area is carefully placed so that it is just a few steps from the main activity – bathing. From the tub you can reach out and take a towel from the heated towel bar, then step out of the bathtub on either side to dry yourself in total comfort. From here, it is just a few steps to the sink to continue your routine before getting dressed.

FOR MORE DETAILS...

Toilets and bidets
SEE PP.34–35

Heating and ventilation
SEE PP.38–39

Wallcoverings SEE P.44

Dual-purpose Bathroom ideas

△ Bathroom-cum-sitting room
Space beneath the window has been fitted with a sofa and plenty of cushions to create a comfortable, quiet place in which to relax and read a book or magazine. It also enables other family members to sit in and catch up on the day's events with the bathtub's occupant.

▽ Bathing Under the Eaves
This converted attic space remains open-plan so that the pitched ceiling and beams can be fully appreciated. Separate zones have been allocated for a breakfast and dressing table, while the bathtub occupies center stage.

△ Washing Clothes in Style
Partitioning off a section of the bathroom to install a washing machine makes good use of the existing plumbing. For the washing area to be an attractive addition to the rest of the bathroom, the machine alcove and storage shelves are painted a vivid blue.

Simple Relaxation ▷
Two floor levels in one room present the opportunity to create a special bedroom-cum-bathroom. The close proximity of the tub to the bed makes it easy to slip effortlessly from one to the other, which is particularly enticing when you are tired or simply want to relax.

CHILDREN'S BATHROOM PLAN

CREATING A BATHROOM that is both fun and safe for young children to use is simple as long as you are aware of a few basic principles when planning and fitting the room. For example, add childproof locks to cupboards, ensure there are no sharp edges around the tub and sink area, choose a nonslip flooring, and have plenty of water toys to keep the users happy.

CHILD'S SEAT
Bolted on to a standard-size toilet, the small seat can be replaced when the child is older.

Standard tub   Storage   Part-enclosed toilet   Wall shelf

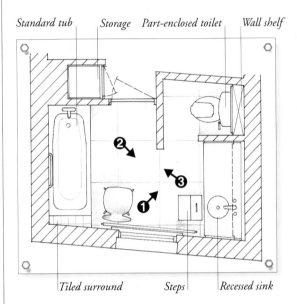

Tiled surround   Steps   Recessed sink

△ BIRD'S-EYE VIEW
The tub and sink sit flush against the walls so that no element juts out that may be bumped. The toilet area is screened off but accessible, and steps help children reach the sink.

INTERNAL ROOM DIMENSIONS:
10ft 4in (3.2m) long
8ft 1in (2.5m) wide

△ ❶ PRIVATE CORNER
The partitioned toilet area offers a degree of privacy for young children, but, because there is no door, they cannot accidentally lock themselves in. Intended for children to learn to use a grown-up toilet independently, this allows adults to easily help if the child needs it.

SHOWER HEAD
Children tend to dislike showers, so a friendly dinosaur head helps to make this activity fun.

FOR MORE DETAILS...

Toilet seats SEE P.35

Storage SEE PP.36–37

Heating and ventilation SEE PP.38–39

Rubber flooring SEE P.43

TILED SURROUND
Grouted ceramic tiles will sustain a regular soaking and are durable.

❷ USING THE SINK ▷
Brushing teeth or washing hands can be difficult when faucets are hard to reach. A step that will not topple over and can be moved when required will encourage children to perform their morning and bedtime routine independently.

WALL CUPBOARDS
Choose a unit that locks to keep toiletries and medicines out of children's reach.

COUNTERTOP
Rounded edges and an easy-clean finish are essential.

LAUNDRY BASKET
A brightly colored fabric laundry basket can be tucked under the counter, out of harm's way.

CHAIR
Install a chair for adults supervising bathtime and towel-drying children sitting on their lap.

WOODEN STEPS
Choose a sturdy but light design that children can move into place.

DESIGN POINTS

■ Provide a laundry basket to encourage children to deal with their dirty clothes rather than leaving them strewn all over the bathroom floor.

■ A cold bathroom will make children grumble and resist baths; warmth, fresh towels, and water toys will go a long way to overcoming their dread.

■ Flooring should be chosen for its resistance to accidental spills and splashes and should be soft and warm enough for children to walk on barefoot.

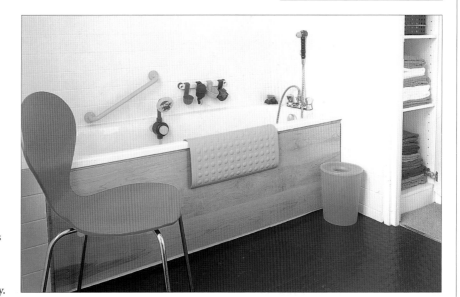

BATH SAFETY ❸ ▷
To make bathtime as safe as possible for young children, choose a bathtub with a curved edged so that little hands can get a grip when climbing in and out of the bathtub. Mount a brightly colored grab bar for children to hold onto when standing up in the tub, and place a rubber mat on the bottom of the bathtub to make it less slippery.

CHILDREN'S BATHROOM IDEAS

△ DEVELOPING SKILLS
With the help of your children, paint murals on ceramic tiles to make bathtime fun. Use cold ceramic paints, which are easy to apply and durable once fully dry.

◁ FUR EFFECT
Add a touch of humor by painting a cow print or tiger print on the side of the bathtub. Alternatively, a mix of bright colors, spots, and squiggles will make it fun to use.

△ CUT-OUT CREATIONS
Cut-out superheroes and TV characters bring instant color to bare walls, while red rubber flooring and red toilet seat, blind, and plumbing appeal to children. Color-coded plastic jars keep soaps and sponges neat.

3-D DESIGN ▷
Clever ideas transform this colorful bathroom into an underwater kingdom children will treasure. All the decorative surfaces are varnished so that they are waterproof and can be wiped clean when necessary.

SHARED BATHROOM PLAN

COMMUNAL BATHROOMS with a shower, a tub, and a double sink unit need not be very large, but they must be well-planned. There should be space around the fixtures so that the user does not feel too cramped, and a plentiful supply of hot water to feed the shower, tub, and sinks so that they can be enjoyed by different members of the family at the same time. An efficient heating and ventilation system to heat the room and extract steam is also essential.

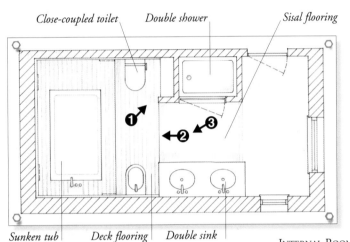

Close-coupled toilet   Double shower   Sisal flooring

Sunken tub   Deck flooring   Double sink

△ **BIRD'S EYE VIEW**
In this large room, two runs of fixtures sit opposite one another along the walls; the double sink and bidet are placed opposite the shower and toilet. The sunken tub, set within a cedarwood platform at the far end of the bathroom, creates an inviting focal point.

INTERNAL ROOM
DIMENSIONS:
8ft 8in (2.7m) wide
17ft 9in (5.5m) long

◁ **① CORNER DETAIL**
This discreet area, tucked around the side of the shower, is practically planned; the bottom shelves keep toilet tissue next to the toilet, while a wall radiator warms towels that are easy to reach when you step out of the tub.

GLASS SHELVING
Space left at the side of the shower is fitted with glass storage shelves.

WALL LIGHTS
Sealed lights are waterproof and shatterproof, making them an ideal choice for this setting next to the bath.

LIFT-UP SECTIONS
A tiled surface below the decking means that the wood planks can be lifted out and the area beneath cleaned.

◁ **② EFFECTIVE LIGHTING**
The simplicity of this two-to-four-person sunken tub benefits from its bright position beneath a clear glass skylight, which can be opened wide on bright days. At night, a far more subtle lighting effect is achieved by recessed wall lights; these cast a soft glow for relaxed, intimate evenings.

SCENTED WOOD
When splashed with water, the cedarwood releases a fabulous woody aroma.

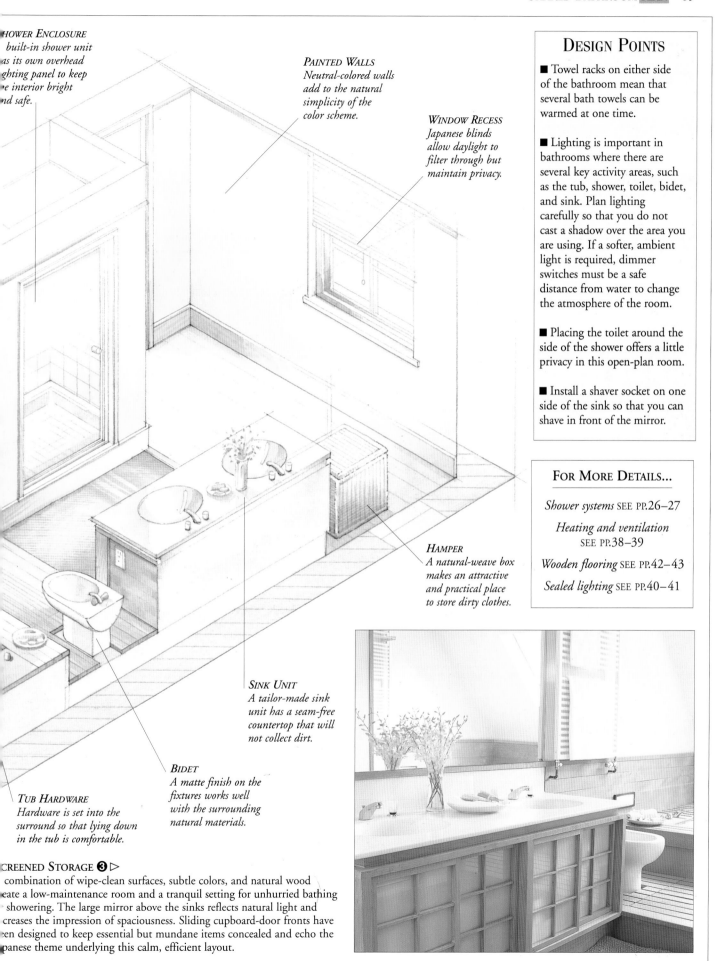

SHOWER ENCLOSURE
*A built-in shower unit
has its own overhead
lighting panel to keep
the interior bright
and safe.*

PAINTED WALLS
*Neutral-colored walls
add to the natural
simplicity of the
color scheme.*

WINDOW RECESS
*Japanese blinds
allow daylight to
filter through but
maintain privacy.*

HAMPER
*A natural-weave box
makes an attractive
and practical place
to store dirty clothes.*

SINK UNIT
*A tailor-made sink
unit has a seam-free
countertop that will
not collect dirt.*

BIDET
*A matte finish on the
fixtures works well
with the surrounding
natural materials.*

TUB HARDWARE
*Hardware is set into the
surround so that lying down
in the tub is comfortable.*

SCREENED STORAGE ❸ ▷

combination of wipe-clean surfaces, subtle colors, and natural wood
create a low-maintenance room and a tranquil setting for unhurried bathing
showering. The large mirror above the sinks reflects natural light and
creases the impression of spaciousness. Sliding cupboard-door fronts have
en designed to keep essential but mundane items concealed and echo the
panese theme underlying this calm, efficient layout.

DESIGN POINTS

■ Towel racks on either side
of the bathroom mean that
several bath towels can be
warmed at one time.

■ Lighting is important in
bathrooms where there are
several key activity areas, such
as the tub, shower, toilet, bidet,
and sink. Plan lighting
carefully so that you do not
cast a shadow over the area you
are using. If a softer, ambient
light is required, dimmer
switches must be a safe
distance from water to change
the atmosphere of the room.

■ Placing the toilet around the
side of the shower offers a little
privacy in this open-plan room.

■ Install a shaver socket on one
side of the sink so that you can
shave in front of the mirror.

FOR MORE DETAILS...

Shower systems SEE PP.26–27

Heating and ventilation
SEE PP.38–39

Wooden flooring SEE PP.42–43

Sealed lighting SEE PP.40–41

Shared Bathroom IDEAS

△ Opposite Corners

Placing the tub and the shower opposite one another ensures that conversations can continue when both are in use. Planned space for bathrobes and essentials has been designed for each user to keep their belongings within easy reach.

△ Angled Layout

A corner bath and shower butted up against one another make full use of the space, allowing two people to use the room in comfort. Sinks placed side by side with storage below keep the area clutter-free.

△ Double Shower

A large double shower unit rather than a single shower and tub may be more suited to your lifestyle. It can save on water consumption and speed up time spent in the bathroom. It can be shared with a partner, or muddy children can be piled in to wash. Choose durable ceramic tiles for the interior, especially if the shower is frequently used.

Space to Move ▷

Although it is possible for two people to share a standard-sized bathroom, it may be cramped. Here, a spare bedroom is converted into a luxuriously large shared bathroom. Space fixtures so that each piece is easy to access. Plan the space to allow for a freestanding bathtub, separate shower unit, and a chair for towels and clothes.

UNUSUAL-SHAPE BATHROOM PLAN

THE INCREASING demands of homeowners for a second bathroom often means that the largest bedroom is divided up or a bathroom is squeezed in under the eaves. Both of these solutions can leave you with an irregular-shaped room with little natural light. Imaginative planning, however, can ensure that the fixtures are well situated and that irregular walls and odd angles are an asset, not a drawback.

ROOF SKYLIGHT
Light filters through a roof panel in each partition, making the bathroom brighter.

MOSAIC TILES
Mosaic, lining the shower area, protects the walls.

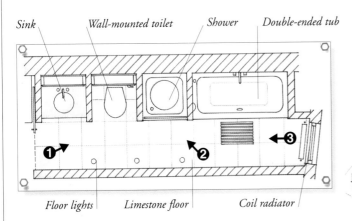

Sink   *Wall-mounted toilet*   *Shower*   *Double-ended tub*

Floor lights   *Limestone floor*   *Coil radiator*

△ **BIRD'S EYE VIEW**
A long, narrow space under the gabled roof has been cleverly divided to create a galley-style bathroom. All the fixtures sit in a row along one wall for an uncomplicated plumbing run, while a corridor along the length of the room connects the different activity zones.

INTERNAL ROOM DIMENSIONS:
5ft 2in (1.6m) wide
15ft 9in (4.9m) long

△ **❶ ALL ON ONE SIDE**
Placing the sink, toilet, shower, and tub along the left-hand side of the room, while keeping the right-hand side of the bathroom free to walk between each item, is inspired planning. Partitions create identities for each activity zone without the need for doors, so the room feels light and spacious.

SLIDING DOOR
A space-saving sliding door opens and closes without interrupting the sink area.

PARTITION
The wall offers privacy while allowing air to flow freely.

FLOOR LIGHTS
Sealed halogen units are safe for bathroom use since they are low-voltage and water-resistant.

SHOWER INTERIOR ❷ ▷

The shower stall stands in the middle of the roof area – where the ceiling is highest – so that there is plenty of room for showering. The stall is subjected to a regular soaking, so the walls are covered in mosaic tiles for a durable finish, which with good door seals prevents water leakage.

ROLLER BLINDS
Blinds take up little space and allow diffused light to pass into the room.

SLOPING CEILING
A tub under the eaves makes good use of space; you sit up without hitting your head.

COIL RADIATOR
Occupying a small floor area, a coil heats the air as it rises.

FOR MORE DETAILS...

Shower and tub hardware
SEE PP.28–29

Wall-mounted toilet SEE P.35

Mosaic wallcovering
SEE P.45

Limestone flooring SEE P.43

▽ ❸ DESIGN DETAIL

Stone flooring is water-resistant and is ideally suited to heavy-wear areas such as the narrow passage between each fixture. Sealed floor lights sunk into the limestone tiles are shatterproof and produce a soft, diffused light that illuminates the length of the walkway, adding character.

STEEL TRIM
Finished in galvanized steel rather than wood, the trim will not deteriorate in damp conditions.

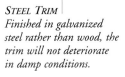

DESIGN POINTS

■ Showers fit into most small and awkward areas, but make sure they are well lit or they can be hazardous.

■ Good ventilation is essential – even more so when space is limited and airflow restricted. Plan the position of the extractor fan opposite the door where it will draw fresh air in.

■ Keep colors and patterns simple in a small bathroom, and avoid fussy hardware.

UNUSUAL-SHAPE BATHROOM IDEAS

△ CORNER SOLUTION
If you do not have the wall space for a standard tub, a corner bathtub may solve the problem. A shower head and curtain rail over the tub mean that it can double up as a shower stall; the curtain can be pulled to one side to let light in.

▽ MEZZANINE FLOOR
Using a good architect will pay dividends when faced with a studio conversion. Here, a high-ceilinged room is divided up to create a spectacular bathroom on the upper level. A tensile-steel structure offers a strong platform for the fixtures.

△ DEEP TUB
A deep tub makes the best use of space in a small bathroom. A tub and shower mixer faucet offers a sit-down shower option. Shelves and a towel make use of the wall space, and an offset sink leaves room for the door to open.

△ IRREGULAR LEVELS
The floor of this bathroom drops deeply into a small recess, making the perfect place to sink a bathtub. Once lying down in the tub, the windows are no threat to privacy. Clear roof panels allow light to flood into this small room.

SUNKEN BATHTUB ▷
Recessing a bathtub into the floor is an imaginative way to create the illusion of space. The underside of the tub is cushioned for protection, and the weight of the marble walls and tiles are taken by the solid floor. Glass blocks replace the window, filtering the light.

PLOT YOUR ROOM

THE STARTING POINT for designing any bathroom is the floor plan and elevations. The following steps will help you measure the room. Then, transfer the dimensions onto graph paper to give scale drawings which you can refer to when planning the layout.

EQUIPMENT
This basic equipment for drawing and measuring will help you record the bathroom's dimensions, service points, and any irregular architectural features. These will determine where you decide to place your bathroom fixtures, radiators, light fixtures, and storage units.

NOTEPAD   TAPE MEASURE

FLOOR DIMENSIONS

Before installing a bathroom, you must have an understanding of the plumbing layout. Check that pipework is in the right place for your choice of toilet, tub, radiator, and sink, and, if not, budget for any plumbing alterations. Familiarize yourself with the shape of the room and the position of windows; these will also dictate the design. Consult the floor plan when choosing furniture to check that items fit into the available space.

❶ SKETCH THE ROOM
Begin by standing in the middle of the room, looking down at the floor. Draw a rough sketch with a soft pencil, starting at the door and working clockwise around the room. Include fixed architectural features.

❷ MEASURE THE FLOOR
Next, plot the dimensions of the room by measuring the total floor area. Place the tape measure across the room and note down the width on your sketch in a colored pen. Ignore any details such as the baseboards at this early stage.

❸ PLOT WALL LENGTH
Next work around the room, measuring each wall length in turn. Remember that not all walls are symmetrical or at right angles to one another, so take care to provide an accurate survey of their lengths.

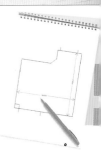

❹ AWKWARD CORNERS
Recesses and projections need careful measuring to ensure that they are correct on the plan. If necessary, take a photograph to keep with the plans to provide a visual guide to irregular shapes, or make a paper template for future use.

❺ PLOT SERVICE POINTS
Plot the position of service points, such as plumbing, electricity, and vent pipe on your plan. Make a note of their distance from any corners. To avoid long unsightly ducting, place the toilet as close as possible to the vent pipe.

❻ CHECK DISTANCES
Note the distances between existing pipe runs for the central heating and water supply so that items will fit when placed side by side. If you need to move the pipes, a plumber will be able to work out the cost from your plan.

WALL ELEVATIONS

Drawing and measuring the elevations is a valuable exercise since it will help you decide whether a sink or toilet can fit beneath a window, or if furniture will obstruct ventilation ducts or radiators. Elevations are useful if you are installing items like a high-level toilet (*see p.34*), since a tall wall is needed for the tank.

❶ RECORD THE HEIGHT
Measure from the floor to the window sill, since some sink and tank designs are higher than average and may not fit the space. Noting the position of the window will also help you plan extra lighting in dark corners.

❷ RECORD DISTANCES
Measure the blank wall space from the window to the nearest corner. Measure the distance from the top of the window to the ceiling cornice to check that curtains will not obstruct the window and reduce the light level.

DRAWING SCALE PLANS

From your sketch survey (created following the steps on the facing page) you have the information you need to work out approximately where to position furniture and fixtures in the room. If you wish to create a more detailed drawing, plot the floor plan and wall elevations to scale on graph paper, using the advice below.

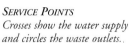

SERVICE POINTS
Crosses show the water supply and circles the waste outlets.

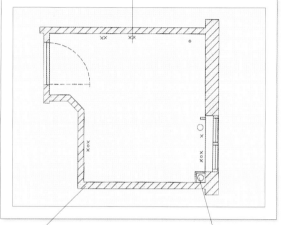

WALLS
Use a narrow border of cross-hatching for internal walls and a thicker border for external.

WASTE STACK
All the waste will drain from this pipe.

YOU WILL NEED
Metric and imperial graph paper is supplied with this book, but you will also need a try square, ruler, pen, pencil, pencil sharpener, and eraser.

◁❶ TRANSFER THE FLOOR PLAN
Taking the precise measurements from your rough sketch, draw the four perimeter walls to scale on graph paper. Use a try square to join corners and straight lines. Next, plot the existing features that are important for planning, such as the waste stack, water supply, door opening, and windows.

❷ DRAW AN ELEVATION ▷
Referring to the measurements on your rough sketch elevations, draw each wall to scale. Mark the hinges, window catches, and door handles to indicate which way they open. Draw in any service pipes to help you decide which alterations may be required for you to achieve your ideal bathroom layout.

❸ OTHER ELEVATIONS ▽
Reserve space on your external wall elevation for a ventilation system, and plan the rest so the room's features are unobstructed.

CORNICE DEPTH
A deep cornice will interrupt a tall tank or cupboard.

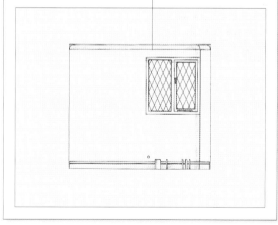

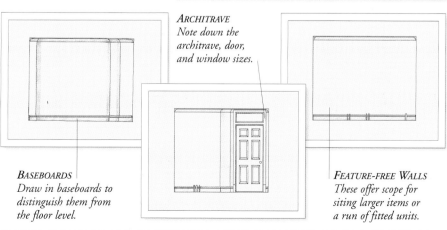

ARCHITRAVE
Note down the architrave, door, and window sizes.

BASEBOARDS
Draw in baseboards to distinguish them from the floor level.

FEATURE-FREE WALLS
These offer scope for siting larger items or a run of fitted units.

PLACE THE FEATURES

HAVING COMPILED A LIST of your preferred fixtures, furniture, and hardware, and mapped out your room plan on graph paper, you should have all the information at your fingertips to be able to work out the best arrangement of features in the bathroom. Try out several different design layouts by placing tracing paper over the scaled-down plan (*see pp.78–79*) and drawing on the elements. You may need to work up several versions and analyze the pros and cons of each before reaching a satisfactory solution.

TRACING PAPER

MASKING TAPE

PEN
SHARPENER
PENCIL
ERASER

TRY SQUARE

RULER

EQUIPMENT ▷
Take the room plan that you have drawn to scale and, using masking tape, stick a sheet of tracing paper over the top. With a soft pencil, draw the features; the ruler and try square will give accurate lines. Plan each new design on a fresh sheet of tracing paper.

DESIGN GUIDELINES

All the elements for the bathroom need to be considered together in order to arrive at a coherent design. When planning your space, bear the following points in mind:

❶ Manufacturers' brochures include the dimensions of fixtures and hardware. Use these precise details to help you draw the items to scale on your plan.

❷ Keeping bathroom pipe runs simple will limit disruption and plumbing costs. If possible, try to place fixtures along adjacent walls so that supply and waste pipes run neatly under the floorboards and cause the minimum disruption and expense.

❸ The position of the toilet is dictated by the fact that it needs to be close to the waste stack, which expels waste into the sewer system. The vent pipe from the toilet must have enough "drop" from the stack in order to discharge solid waste. Vent pipes are also wider than waste-water pipes and look best hidden behind ducting to be less obtrusive.

REJECTED PLANS

Arriving at a well-planned, ergonomic design takes time. Look at the position of each item on the plan and imagine what it would be like, in practice, to use the facilities where you have placed them. Remember that space is needed around each item for ease of use, and fixtures near the door must not restrict access.

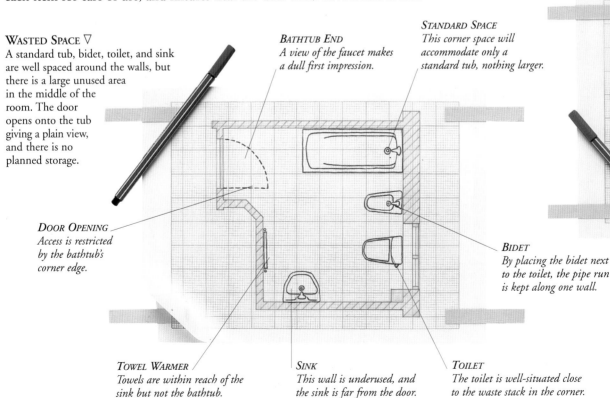

WASTED SPACE ▽
A standard tub, bidet, toilet, and sink are well spaced around the walls, but there is a large unused area in the middle of the room. The door opens onto the tub giving a plain view, and there is no planned storage.

BATHTUB END
A view of the faucet makes a dull first impression.

STANDARD SPACE
This corner space will accommodate only a standard tub, nothing larger.

DOOR SWING
The door will open onto the person using the basin closest to the door.

DOOR OPENING
Access is restricted by the bathtub's corner edge.

BIDET
By placing the bidet next to the toilet, the pipe run is kept along one wall.

BIDET
Wall sp... on eith... side is wasted.

TOWEL WARMER
Towels are within reach of the sink but not the bathtub.

SINK
This wall is underused, and the sink is far from the door.

TOILET
The toilet is well-situated close to the waste stack in the corner.

SUCCESSFUL PLAN

Having assessed the advantages and disadvantages of each bathroom plan, and worked out the most ergonomic configuration of fixtures and other features, plot the most successful design onto graph paper in ink pen. You are now ready to consider design details, such as your wallcovering, flooring, and lighting needs.

SINGLE SINK
The sink is unobstructed by a radiator or tub.

CORNER BATHTUB
Space around the tub makes it easy to climb in and out.

BIDET
Placed next to the toilet, this is easy to use and plumbing is simple.

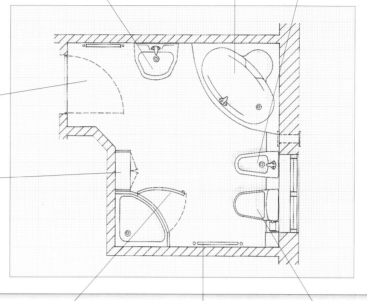

DOOR SWING
Access is unrestricted and offers a good view of all the bathroom's facilities.

STORAGE
Towels and toiletries are kept on open shelving with cleaning products stored behind lockable doors at the base.

PERFECT SOLUTION ▷
The curved shower echoes the shape of the corner tub opposite, while a built-in unit stores essentials neatly, creating a bathroom that looks luxurious and is a pleasure to use. Two radiators, one by the door and one next to the shower, keep the room warm.

SHOWER DOOR
The curved shower door opens into the room.

TOWEL RADIATOR
Warm towels are in reach of the shower.

TOILET
There is room to sit in comfort on the toilet.

LACK OF SPACE
Space around the sinks is very limited. There is insufficient elbow room for two people to use the area at the same time.

CROWDED FIXTURES ▽
Replacing the standard bathtub with a corner tub has made better use of wall space, but the door area is still crowded. By relocating the other fixtures, there is now room for a shower.

INTERRUPTED USE
The sink is much too close to the bidet and bathroom door for it to be functional.

CRAMPED POSITION
Lack of leg room on either side of the bidet makes it uncomfortable to use.

CORNER BATHTUB
The corner tub frees up more bathroom wall space by cutting into the area in the center of the room.

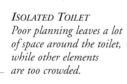

ISOLATED TOILET
Poor planning leaves a lot of space around the toilet, while other elements are too crowded.

DOOR OPENING
The sink is too close to the door, restricting access.

RADIATOR
A corner position restricts warm air circulation.

NO STORAGE PROVISION
By changing the orientation of the bathtub and adding a second sink, the wall space to the left of the door is better used but cramped. The tub doubles up as a shower, and while the bidet and toilet are well spaced, cupboards for towels, toilet paper, and toiletries have been overlooked.

SHOWER
The corner of the shower juts out into the room, and there is no towel bar nearby.

TOILET
Close to the waste stack, the toilet leaves room next to the tub for a radiator.

PLANNING DETAIL

NOW THAT THE BATHROOM LAYOUT has been resolved, you can start choosing details such as fixtures, colors, cupboard finishes, wallcoverings, flooring, lighting, and hardware that match your bathroom needs. Apart from the initial purchase price of items, take into account the total cost of the plumbing and installation and how long the work will take, then plan accordingly.

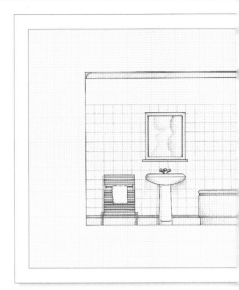

◁ **COLLECT PICTURES**
Decorating and lifestyle magazines can provide you with inspiration. Cut out fixtures and bathrooms that interest you and note down the addresses and telephone numbers of suppliers.

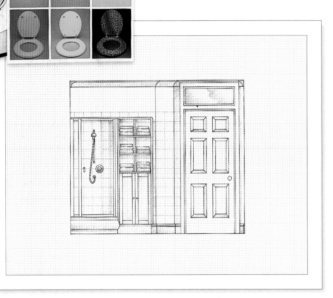

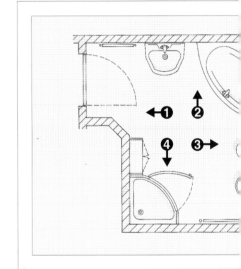

△ **❶ SHOWER AND STORAGE AREA**
Draw in the fixtures and hardware to help you visualize how they will fit into the space you have allocated. Here, the storage unit has been built to the same height as the shower so the top of the wall is free and the room appears taller. The storage unit has been divided up into open shelving and cupboards to help organize products.

◁ **PRODUCT BROCHURES**
Collect manfacturers' brochures so that you have full details of their line of products. Specialized bathroom showrooms should also be able to provide product information. Keep this literature at hand when planning the room: it contains the dimensions, styles, color choices, and price lists.

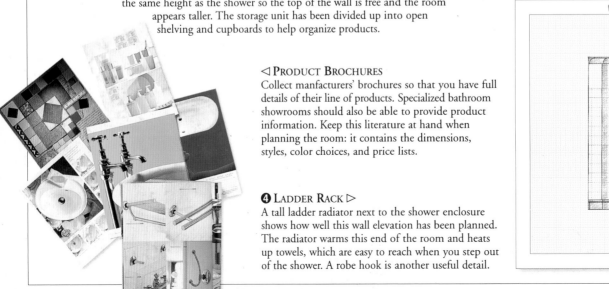

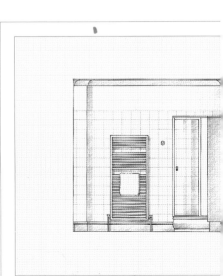

❹ **LADDER RACK** ▷
A tall ladder radiator next to the shower enclosure shows how well this wall elevation has been planned. The radiator warms this end of the room and heats up towels, which are easy to reach when you step out of the shower. A robe hook is another useful detail.

MATERIAL SAMPLES ▷
Collect samples showing fixture colors, flooring materials, and wallcoverings. Keep a collection of your favorite items to help you make your style decisions.

◁ ❷ SINK ELEVATION
The tub and towel radiator leave "elbow room" around the sink area for performing activities such as shaving and applying makeup. A mirror above the sink area helps with these tasks and reflects light into the room from the window. Install a shaver socket close to the sink and mirror when other electrical work is done.

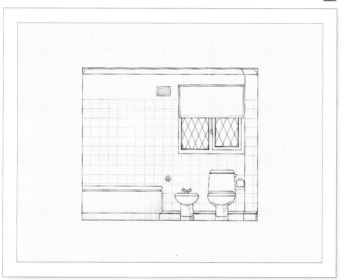

▽ FLOOR PLAN
Number the walls on your floor plan and copy the same numbers onto the corresponding elevation, so that you can see at a glance exactly where each element is placed within the room.

△ ❸ WALL DETAIL
Plot the tub, bidet, and toilet elevation to check that there is plenty of leg room on either side of the fixtures and that there is space behind for ducting to hide the wide vent pipe. Details such as a toilet paper holder and towel hook are also planned at a suitable height, as is an unobtrusive extractor grille for this outside wall.

COLOR SCHEMES ▷
Although color choice is a matter of personal taste, bear in mind that pale shades will make a bathroom appear more spacious while dark tones absorb light and make it look smaller. Remember that different surface finishes affect the quality of light. High-gloss paint finishes and shiny tiles increase reflections and glare while matte finishes diffuse light.

WHAT NEXT?

■ When you have a clear idea of what you want, take your finished design to a bathroom showroom, plumber, or design company to help put all your ideas into action. If structural work is required you may need to contact an architect. He or she will be able to advise you on planning regulations or health and safety restrictions.

■ It is important to plan the order of work, since a cast of builders, plumbers, electricians, fitters, tilers, and decorators may be involved. The work should proceed as follows: structural changes, electrical wiring, plumbing and fitting of fixtures and cupboards, wall tiling, flooring, and finally decoration. The exception to this is if you want fitted carpets, which should be installed last.

■ Delivery times for fixtures and hardware can be long, so check that the goods you have ordered will be delivered in your time frame. When they arrive, make sure that they are as ordered and undamaged.

BUDGET TIPS

■ It is easy to go over budget when choosing both your fixtures and hardware, and it's very difficult to find cheap alternatives of similar quality. For this reason, ask about discounted floor samples from showrooms, which can be great bargains.

■ A bathroom tiled from floor to ceiling can be prohibitively expensive, but, if this is your preferred finish, opt for pure white or plain-colored tiles, which are cheaper than patterned tiles. To prevent the bathroom from looking too clinical, use the more expensive patterned or colored tiles in a single border to add interest.

USEFUL ADDRESSES

The following directory of useful names and addresses will help you furnish and equip your bathroom. Many have brochures or extensive catalogs available free or for a small charge. If you are considering structural work, it is advisable to consult your builder or an architect.

BATHROOM SPECIALISTS

AMERICAN CHINA INC.
6615 West Boston Street
Chandler, AZ 85226.
Tel: (800) 359-3261
Tubs, toilets, and sinks. Call for brochure and the locations of local distributors.

AMERICAN STANDARD, INC.
PO Box 6820
One Centennial Plaza
Piscataway, NJ 08855
Tel: (800) 752-6292
Tubs, toilets, sinks, faucets, and hardware. Call for catalog and product information.

THE ANTIQUE HARDWARE STORE
19 Buckingham Plantation Drive
Bluffton, SC 29910
Tel: (800) 422-9982
Bathroom antiques, including fixtures, hardware, and accessories. Call for catalog.

AQUAWARE AMERICA INC.
1 Selleck Street
Norwalk, CT 06855
Tel: (800) 527-4498
Shower and tub surrounds, enclosures, and doors.

BROAN MANUFACTURING CO.
926 West State Street
Hartford, WI 53027
Tel: (800) 548-0790
Built-in hair dryers. Call for store locations.

CRATE & BARREL
Tel: (888) 249-4158
Hampers, shower curtains, bath rugs, mats, scales, and other accessories. Call for catalog.

DELTA FAUCET
55 East 111th Street
Indianapolis, IN 46280
Tel: (800) 345-DELTA
A range of bathroom hardware, including shower heads. Call for product literature.

DUPONT CORIAN®
Barley Mill Plaza
PO Box 80012
Wilmington, DE 19880-0012
Tel: (800) 426-7426
Manufacturer of ready-to-install shower-stall kits, tub-and-shower surround kits, bathroom counter surfaces, and sinks. Call for product information and literature.

FEENY MANUFACTURING CO.
PO Box 191
Muncie, IN 47308
Tel: (800) 899-6535
Cosmetic drawers, hampers, grooming racks, and other bathroom organizers. Call for product information and store locations.

FINLANDIA SAUNA
14010B S.W. 72nd Avenue
Portland, OR 97224-0088
Tel: (800) 354-3342
Fax: (503) 684-1120
Call for product information.

GENERAL MARBLE
350 North Generals Boulevard
Lincolnton, NC 28092
Tel: (800) 432-4114
Manufacturers of cultured marble sinks. Call for the locations of local sink retailers.

HOLD EVERYTHING
3250 Van Ness Avenue
San Francisco, CA 91409
Tel: (800) 421-2264
Storage items for the bathroom. Call for catalog and store locations.

HOME DEPOT
Corporate Offices
2727 Paces Ferry Road
Atlanta, GA 30339
Tel: (770) 433-8211
Nationwide chain of home supply stores. Call for the addresses of retail outlets.

IKEA
Tel: (800) 434-4532 Regional
Tel: (410) 931-8940 East Coast
Tel: (818) 912-1199 West Coast
Textiles, towel rails, bath cabinets, and other accessories; call for catalog and store locations.

JACUZZI WHIRLPOOL BATH
2121 North California Boulevard
Suite 475
Walnut Creek, CA 94596
Tel: (800) 678-6889
Whirlpool baths, shower systems, spas, and faucets. Call for product literature and the locations of retailers.

KOHLER CO.
44 Highland Drive
Kohler, WI 53044
Tel: (800) 4-KOHLER
website: www.kohlerco.com
Toilets, bidets, sinks, tubs, steam baths, saunas, shower heads, and hardware. Call for catalog and the locations of local showrooms.

KOLSON INC.
653 Middle Neck Road
Great Neck, NY 11023
Tel: (516) 487-1224
website: www.kolson.com
Multiple lines of bidets, toilets, sinks, and tubs. Call for catalog and orders.

NORTHSTAR ACRYLIC DESIGNS
PO Box 370350
Denver, CO 80237
Tel: (888) 225-8827
Victorian-style bathroom products, such as clawfoot and slipper tubs, reproduction faucets, and pedestal sinks. Call for catalog.

PAMCO KITCHEN AND BATH ACCENTS
PO Box 7538
Laguna Niguel, CA 92607
Tel: (714) 493-0214
Towel warmers. Call for product information and the locations of retailers.

POTTERY BARN
Mail Order Department
PO Box 7044
San Francisco, CA 94120-7044
Tel: (800) 922-5507
Accessories such as medicine chests, shower caddies, and shaving mirrors. Call for catalog.

THE RALPH LAUREN HOME COLLECTION
1185 Avenue of the Americas
New York, NY 10036
Tel: (212) 642-8700
Towels, wallpaper. Call for locations of retailers.

RESTORATION HARDWARE
15 Coche Road
Suite J
Corte Madera, CA 94925
Tel: (800) 762-1005
Edwardian reproduction faucets and fixtures. Call for store locations.

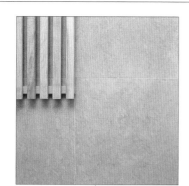

RUNTAL NORTH AMERICA
187 Knack Road
PO Box 8278
Ward Hill, MA 01835
Tel: (800) 526-2621
Towel warmers and decorative radiators. Call for product literature and the locations of retailers.

SEARS CATALOG
Tel: (800) 948-8800
Catalog includes towels, shower curtains, bathroom racks, and more. Nationwide chain of stores carries hardware, showers, and toilets.

SIMON'S HARDWARE & BATH
421 3rd Avenue
New York, NY 10016
Tel: (888) 2-SIMONS
Marble, stone, and ceramic tiles. Faucets and fixtures. Call for catalog and orders.

SUNFLOWER SHOWERHEAD COMPANY
PO Box 4218-K
Seattle, WA 98104
Tel: (206) 722-1232
Fax: (206) 722-1321
Brass and chrome shower heads. Call for brochure.

SUNRISE SPECIALTY CO.
5530 Doyle Street
Emeryville, CA 94608
Tel: (800) 444-4280
Toilets. Call for product literature.

SUSSMAN LIFESTYLE GROUP
(Mr. Steam/ Mr. Sauna/Warmatowel)
4320 34th Street
Long Island City, NY 11101
Tel: (800) 767-8326
Website: www.Mr.Steam.com
Call for product literature and the locations of showrooms.

TREASURE CHEST CUSTOM AQUARIA
2970 Old Forge Road
Waynesboro, PA 17268
Tel: (718) 762-4546
In-wall installation kits for aquariums. Mail and phone orders.

WATERWARE, INC.
15 West 81st Street
New York, NY 10024
Tel: (212) 874-1900
Vinyl shower curtains, plastic throw pillows for the tub, frames made to hang on bathroom surfaces, and other specialty items. Call for the locations of retailers.

WATERWORKS
29 B Sugarhollow Road
Danbury, CT 06810
Tel: (800) 899-6757
Hardware. Call for a catalog.

WALLS AND FLOORS

CROSSVILLE TILE COMPANY
PO Box 1168
Crossville, TN 38557
Tel: (615) 485-2110
Stone tiles, wall tiles, and architectural moldings. Call for catalog.

LAUFEN CERAMIC TILE
PO Box 6600
Tulsa, OK 74156-0600
Tel: (800) 758-8453
Call for brochure and the locations of local distributors.

MANNINGTON RESILIENT FLOORS
PO Box 30
Salem, NJ 08079
Tel: (800) 356-6787
Vinyl flooring. Call for product literature and the locations of local retailers.

NATIONAL BLIND AND WALLPAPER FACTORY
400 Galleria #400
Southfield, MI 48034
Tel: (800) 477-8000
Wallpapers and coverings. Phone orders.

NATIONAL ASSOCIATION

NATIONAL KITCHEN AND BATH ASSOCIATION
687 Willow Grove Street
Hackettstown, NJ 07840
Tel: (800) 843-6522
National association of kitchen and bathroom designers and manufacturers of kitchen and bathroom products.

LIGHTING

BULBMAN
630 Sunshine Lane
Reno, NV 89502
Tel: (800) 648-1163
Fax: (800) 548-6216
Wholesale lighting distributors.

GOLDEN VALLEY LIGHTING
274 Eastchester Drive
High Point, NC 27276
Tel: (800) 735-3377
Specialized and general bathroom lighting. Call for catalog.

OUTWATER PLASTICS INDUSTRIES
PO Box 403
Wood-ridge, NJ 07075
Tel: (800) 631-8375
Manufacturers of lighting products, including shower lights. Phone orders.

TASK LIGHTING CORPORATION
PO Box 1090
910 East 25th Street
Kearney, NE 68848
Tel: (800) 445-6404
Tel: (308) 236-6707
Tel: (308) 234-9401
Designer and manufacturer of lighting systems.

INDEX

ACKNOWLEDGMENTS

AUTHOR'S ACKNOWLEDGMENTS

There are many people to thank for their hard work and assistance in producing this book: all those who allowed us into their homes to photograph their bathrooms, and the team at Dorling Kindersley whose interest and enthusiasm made the book a pleasure to write. Thanks first to Mary-Clare Jerram and Charlotte Davies for offering the marvelous opportunity to write *Bathroom* and to the Editor, Bella Pringle, who deserves much credit for her skill, dedication, and encouragement. Thanks to Sharon Moore and Clive Hayball who worked tirelessly on the design and layout. Thanks also to Richard Lee, whose beautiful illustrations and room plans have brought life to the practical drawings.

Thanks to Isobel Coomber, John Laughton, and Robin Levien from the Ideal-Standard team and Leftley Bros Ltd for their support and help, and to my mother for entertaining the children when away on location and meetings – no mean feat.

Finally, a special thank you must go to my husband Nelson who has juggled his career, the children, and menagerie to provide me with uninterrupted hours of writing and still found time to read drafts and offer ideas.

PUBLISHER'S ACKNOWLEDGMENTS

Dorling Kindersley would like to thank Ally Ireson for picture research, Hilary Bird for the index, Shani Zion for additional styling, and Andrew Nash for design assistance. We would like to thank the architects whose plans appear in the book: Plan pp.49–49 Ken Rorrison, Bushcow Henley, 27–29 Whitfield Street, London, W1P 5RB, 0171 379 6391; Plan pp.68–69 Dale Loth Architects, 1 Cliff Road, London, NW1 9AJ, 0171 485 4003; Plan pp.72–73 Joyce Owens, Azman Owens Architect, 109 Clifton Street, London, EC2 4LD, 0171 739 8404.

Special thanks to Chris Thiede of Kohler Co., Kohler, WI for help with terminology, and to Audrey Hettinger and Debbie Richards of the Kohler Design Center.

We are indebted to the following individuals who generously allowed us to photograph in their homes: Richard Blair-Oliphant; Sheila Fitzjones; Samantha Harrison; Richard and Pauline Lay; John Pemberton; Sharon Reed and William Sargent.

We would like to thank the following companies for allowing us to photograph in their showrooms and showhomes: Alternative Plans 31bl, 31tr, 33tr, 33br, 33bc, 33bl, 35tl, 36 bl, 36cr; C.P. Hart 12b, 22c, 26c, 29tl, 30bl, 31tl, 32t, 32b, 32cr, 34bl, 37br, 38tr, 38br, 43tl, 44br, 45tc, 45bl, 45br.; Leftley Bros Ltd 78–79; Original Bathrooms 10t, 23br, 29bl, 35cr, 37tl, 37bl, 42tr; Sitting Pretty 30t, 32cl, 34r, 35bcr; The Water Monopoly 9t, 16t, 25br, 25cr, 29c, 87br, 88; West One 24cl, 24cr, 25tr, 26bl, 27tl, 27 tr, 28bl, 28cr, 28tr, 29tr, 29cr, 29cl, 29bc, 31br, 33t, 33cl, 33cr, 35cl, 35bcl, 35tr, 41bc.

We would also like to thank the following individuals and companies who lent us items for photography: Alternative Plans; Aston Matthews; Bisque Radiators 38bl; Bobo 35br; Christy Towels; Cologne & Cotton; Descamps; Fiona Craig-McFeely; Habitat; The Holding Company; Innovations; Muji; Natural Products; Newman Tonks Architectural Hardware; Smith & Nephew; The Pier; Pru Bury; Mr Tomkinson Carpets; The Source; Yves Delorme, Ever Trading.

ARTWORK

Room artworks by Richard Lee.
Ergonomic diagrams by David Ashby.

PHOTOGRAPHY

All photographs by Jake Fitzjones except:
Andy Crawford 17r, 19t, 29br, 35br, 37tr, 38bl, 39tr, 39c, 43bl, 43br, 45tl, 76–77, 80–81, 82–83, 86br.
Earl Carter/Belle/Arcaid (Designer: Christian Liagre) 50bl; David Churchill/Arcaid (Architect: Elspeth Beard) 74b; Mike Crockett/Elizabeth Whiting & Associates (Designer: Fiona Cowan) 75; Michael Dunne/Elizabeth Whiting & Associates 66b; Andreas von Einsiedel/National Trust Picture Library 6tl, Andreas von Einsiedel/ Elizabeth Whiting & Associates 74tr; Aki Furudate (Architect: Bramante Architects) 40br; Chris Gascoigne/View (Architect: Simon Conder) 25cl; Dennis Gilbert/View (Architect: Rick Mather) 40tl, (Architect: Bernhard Blauel) 51, (Architect: AHMM) 70cr; Rodney Hyett/ Elizabeth Whiting & Associates 45bc, 74tl; IMS/Camera Press 54tr, 66tr; Simon Kenny/ Belle/Arcaid (Designer: Andrew Nimmo & Annabel Lahz) 74cr; Suomen Kuvapalvelu/ Camera Press 44cl; John Edward Linden/Arcaid (Architect: John Newton) 14–15, (Architect: Julian Powell Tuck) 54tl; Living/Camera Press 58tl; Nadia Mackenzie (Designer Francois Gilles/IPL Interiors) 50tl, (Owner: Paula Pryke) 55, (The Water Monopoly) 66tl; Marianne Majerus (Architect: Barbara Weiss) 70t; Simon McBride (Designer: Kaffe Fasset) 42tl, (Owner: Merete Steinboch) 70–71; James Mortimer/ National Trust Picture Library 6–7; Ian Parry/Abode 58tr, 59; David Parmiter 58br; Spike Powell/ Elizabeth Whiting & Associates 54bl; Jo Reid and John Peck (Architect: Simon Conder) 27bl; Elizabeth Whiting & Associates 70bl; SchonerWohnen/ Camera Press 62tl, 66–67; Friedholm Thomas/ Elizabeth Whiting & Associates 62bl; Petrina Tinslay/Arcaid (Designer: Phil & Jackie Staub) 63; Henry Wilson/Interior Archive (Designer: Patrick Jefferson) 58bl.

The following companies kindly lent us photographs: Antique Baths of Ivybridge 25tl; Jacuzzi UK 24bl; Armitage Shanks 8tc; Ideal-Standard 22tr; Dimplex 39tc; Jaga 39tl; Shires 23tr; Lefroy Brooks 23bl; Mira 29tc; Myson 39cl; Novatec 41tl; Showerlux 22cr, 27bl; Twyfords 35bl; Vent-Axia 39bl, bc.

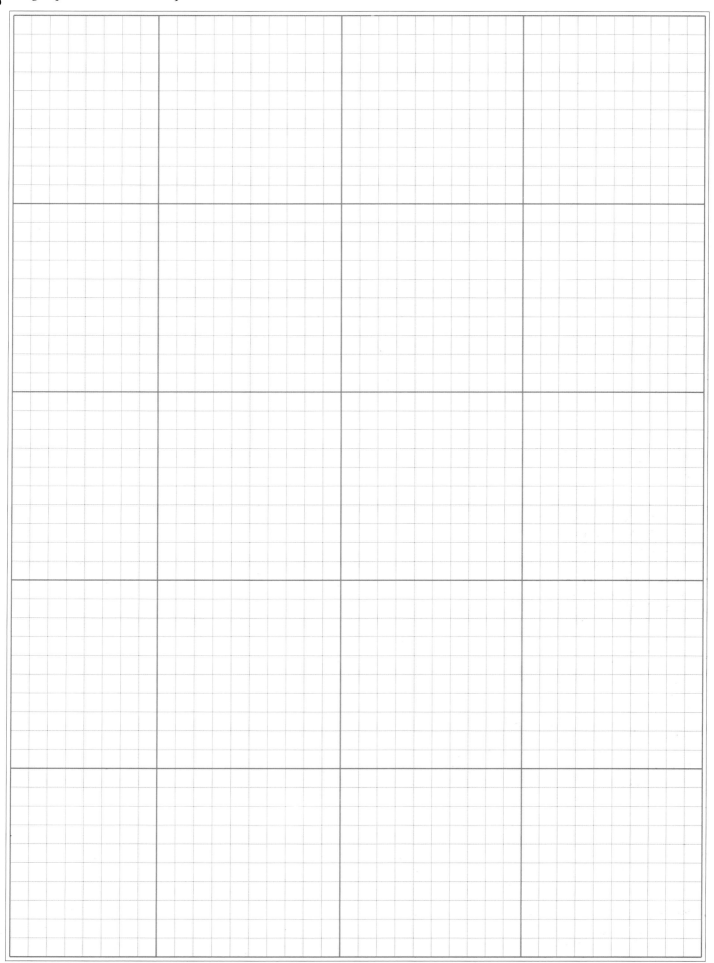

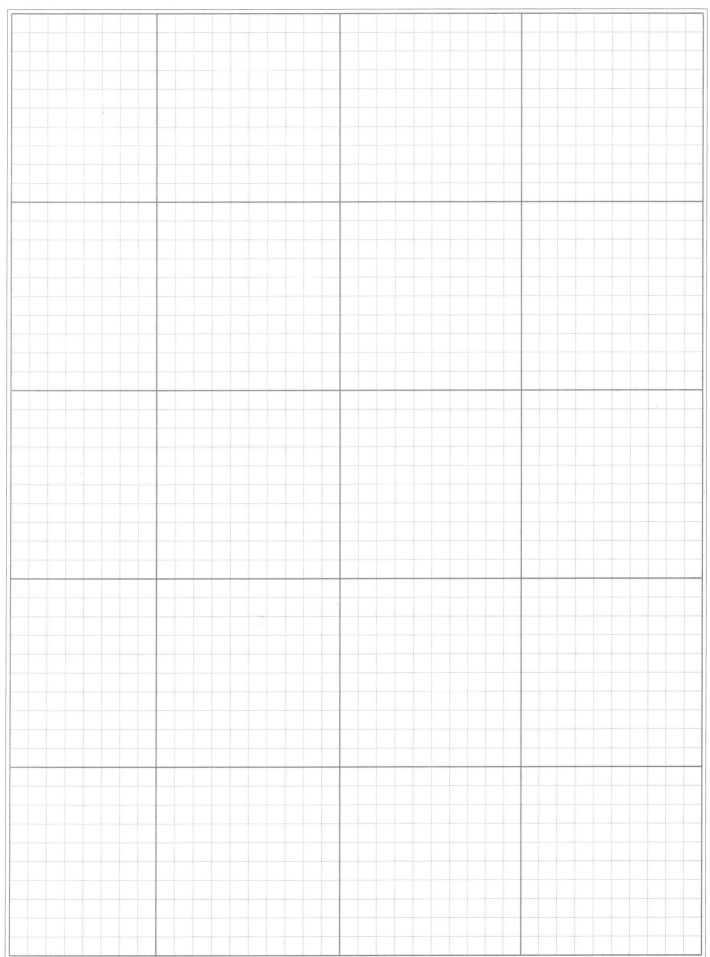

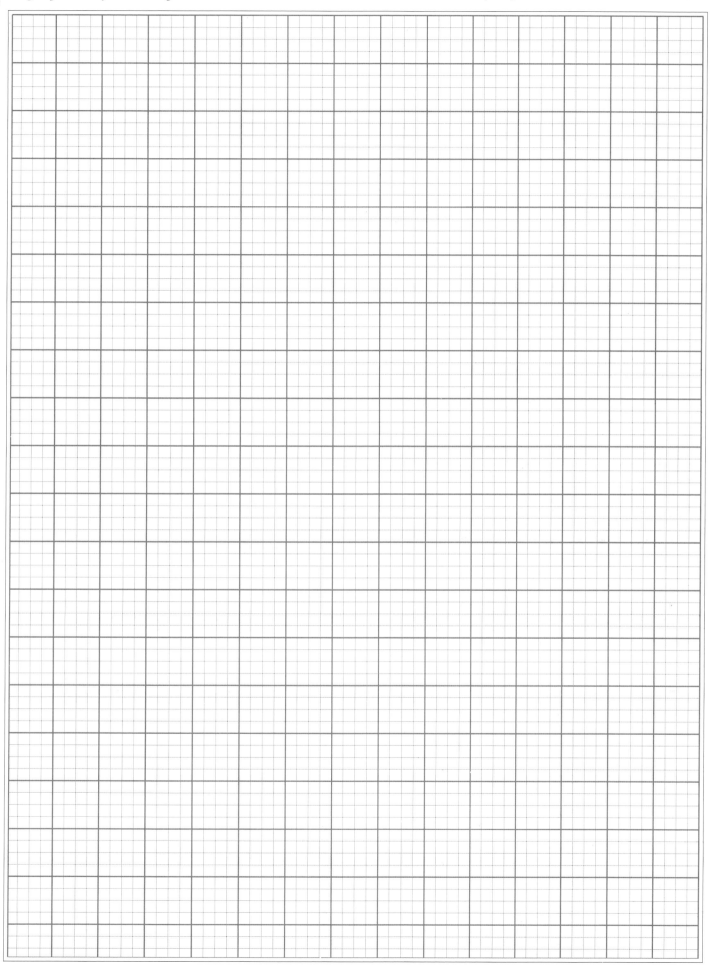

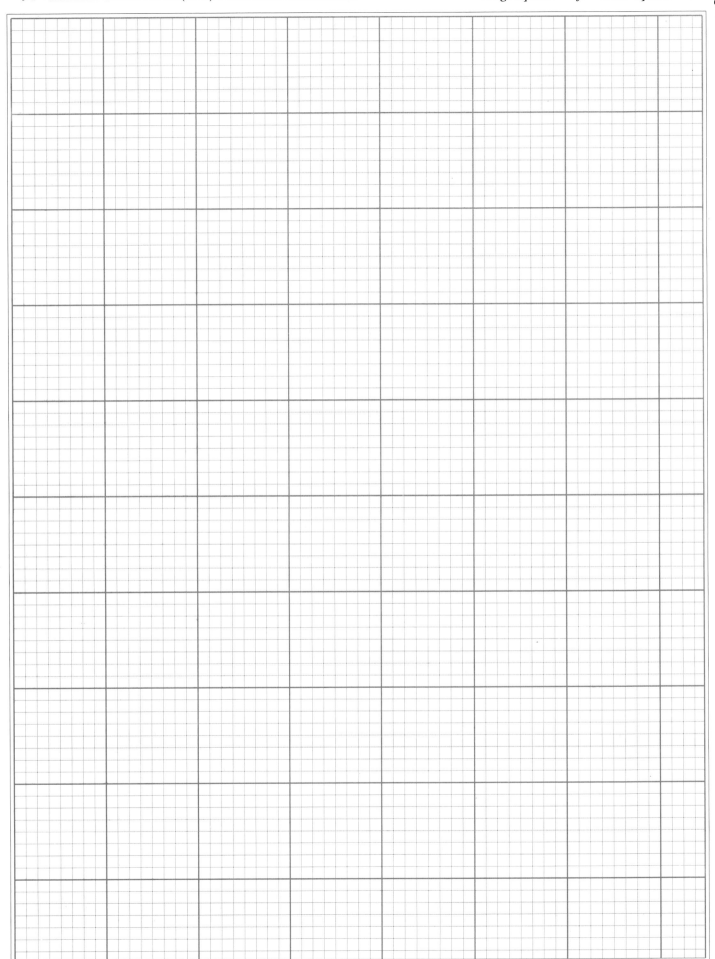

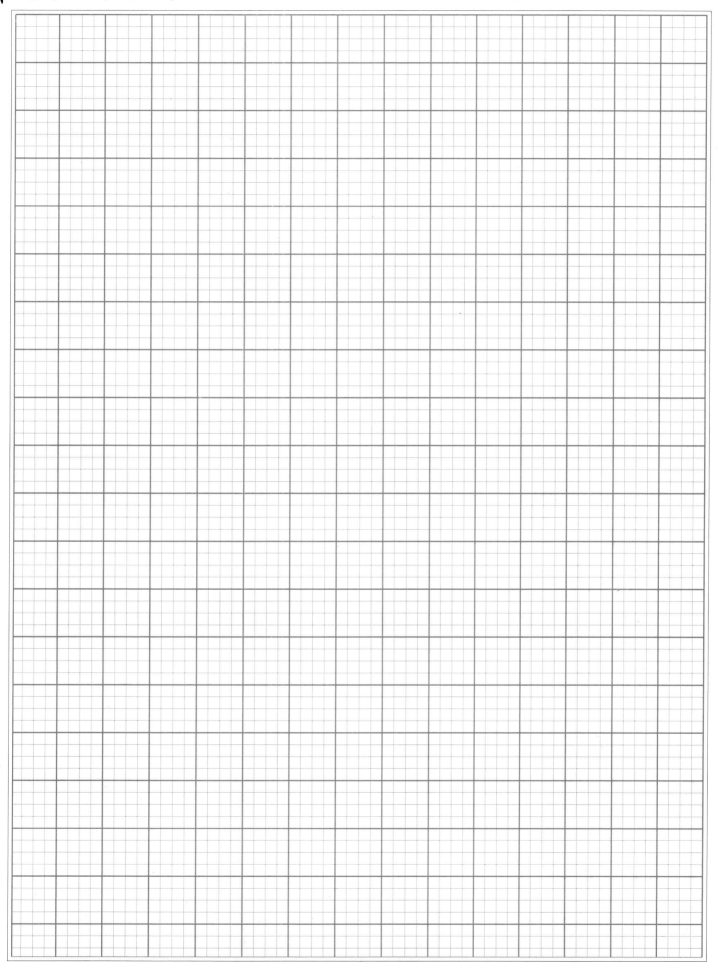